BE
The Living Tree

From Root to Fruit
You are Divine

by
KATHERINE TORRES, Ph.D., D.D.

International Standard Book Number: 1-885015-11-9

Front Cover Design: Jenny Richards
Front Cover Art: Zim Zimmermann

Published by:
Transpersonal Development
1440 S. Orange Ave., #100
El Cajon, CA 92020
800-499-2353

ALSO BY KATHERINE TORRES, PH.D, D.D.:

SOUL MAGIC, Understanding Your Journey

THE FACES OF WOMANSPIRIT, A Celtic Moon Journey

THE FACES OF WOMANSPIRIT, Sweet Mystery

THE FACES OF WOMANSPIRIT, A Celtic Oracle of Avalon

THE FACES OF WOMANSPIRIT COLORING BOOK

Whether you are out on a limb, swimming through confusion, walking on edge, or falling into the abyss, you are Rooted in Source. In ancient and present time, Source is compared to a Tree and we are the Living Aspects of the Tree.

Source is the Seed of All Life and can be compared to the seed of a tree. The seed of a tree is planted in soil and covered with the invaluable minerals of the land as it gestates. In this womb of richness, the movement of life within the seed occurs. In a descending urge, the root bursts out and establishes its foundation for growth. After another period of time, the seed ascends and stretches above the containment of the Earth's mantle. A trunk, a bit fragile at first, begins the next level of the tree's ascent, reaching for the Sun. As it strengthens, it releases limbs, and leaves begin to bud. Further reaching to the light and resting in the night, buds of flowers and delicate petals, often aromatic, spread out to reveal the beauty of growth. If this is a tree of fruit, another spurt of energy occurs and the fruit emerges.

Each point of the journey of growth represent pieces and parts of the Whole, and pieces and parts of ourselves. The pieces are never different from the whole tree, though they may look like it. This lack of difference can be revealed by a scientist. When given a piece of the seed, trunk, limb, leaf, flower and fruit, a scientist can dissect each piece and find the same DNA in every part of the Tree. So it is with each of us: we are the Living Tree, an aspect of Source, expressing through growth as we seek the Light. Our Flowers and the Fruit carry more seeds and the continuum of life is carried on...same DNA... same Source – The Living Tree.

Acknowledgments

The development of this book took many years, many students, clients, and a delightful woman, Jenny, to make me cross the threshold and finish writing it. Her encouragement turned to support as it is her service in book designing that has brought the publishing of this work to life. I am ever grateful for the people who have allowed me to share this wisdom and continue to ask for more. To all of my students, thank you very much. Chuck, Celeste and Barbara, thanks for reading this rendition! And Roger Reimer, thanks for you wonderful copy editing and letting me know you could use the philosophy for your life!

Quiet contemplation and active dedication to a computer caused hours of separation from my husband. Even though 20 feet away, he often realized I was "unreachable" during the times I sat at my computer. Al, thank you for carrying such an attitude of support that offers me the opportunity to continue doing my soul-work. Even now, in the heavenly tree you help me.

To the One Source, I owe my greatest Gratitude! I am forever satiated, allured by Your Intelligence, and graced by Your love. May this book be but a small reflection of Your gift to the consciousness of humanity.

Table of Contents

TABLE OF ILLUSTRATIONS

Introduction

Imagine sitting under a huge Oak tree on a hot summer day with your spine resting against its trunk enjoying the shade provided by lush leaves on a bough and coolness soothing your body as the wind ruffles a wisp or two of air. Nice feeling. In your imagination, relax, open to a vision of a book of Universal Wisdom and promptly fall into contemplation and know: The Tree of Life releases insights, and this book will help you discover them.

I imagine this scenario often and set about contemplating the Universe, and particularly the philosophy of the Tree of Life. I easily create a vision of myself, or a major Celtic figure, the god Odin, hanging upside down on a tree. Storytellers reveal he hung upside down on a branch of a Yggdrasil (Yew Tree) and received All Wisdom. I also remember the story of Buddha sitting under a Bodhi Tree. He, too, received All Wisdom and was called The *Enlightened One* because he soaked up the knowledge from the meditative state while he was aligned with the spine of the tree. I also envision myself imitating him, as well—setting the stage for mystical learning. As a Qabalist, I believe that by studying, observing and contemplating the wisdom of the Qabalah, known as the study of the *Tree of Life*, I can decode Wisdom of the Universe. So can you.

Students, scientists, intellectuals and intuits all want to know about the Tree of Life. Charles Darwin sought the Universal Tree of Life in order to reveal that a common ancestry existed. He believed that everything evolved from one Primordial field of energy. Does it? As I contemplate all of this, while sitting under a tree, I question, "Will this California Oak allow me, or anyone, to get so connected with its roots, and the Life Force within it, that one can receive All Wisdom and know the Primordial Source?"

Though Charles Darwin did not find his Universal Tree of Life, seekers continue to discover the mystical and mysterious Tree – The Living Tree of Source! As they search and study one branch at a time, they uncover the Great Mystery and discover . . . Everyone and Everything is the Living Tree. Are you one of the seekers that continues to unfold the reality that each individual is a part of the Living Tree? I feel you must be or you would not have been drawn to this book. As a person questing for more knowledge of the Tree of Life, I know you are pursuing the desire to know your association with the Creator and how much you may be One with Source. This study provides a means to understand this association.

The Living Tree is Source – Universal Consciousness living in all. Source carries many names: God, Goddess, Divine Mind, Holy of Holy, Allah, Abba, Aima, Tao, Brahma, Divine Human, and so forth. Through contemplation, observation, and inner reflection, you can uncover the wisdom of Universal Consciousness. There is a reality to root up: The Living Tree exists within and there are ways to decode the inner truth and wisdom encoded in the roots and branches of your cellular tree.

As you read this book, you will be inspired to see the existence of Source within you. You will discover how you are the subsistence of All Wisdom as the Living Tree emerges, branch by branch, leaf by leaf within your personal awareness. You will recognize the effect of your living tree as you grow, flower, fruit, and are fed from the wisdom of your succulent inner self. As you harvest from your inner knowing, you will recognize the knowledge you cultivate and the greater quality of life you exude by releasing the Essential Essence of You from the core of your wisdom-base, the Root of your Tree.

This is not just an illusionary promise. It will not come as instantly as sitting under a tree or hanging upside down from a limb. However, the unfolding of personal wisdom, and ultimately, Universal Wisdom will come. How? Through contemplation and awareness of what is happening in your life that reflects this truth. By learning of the structure of Source Consciousness called *The Tree of Life*, you will understand that this is not just a philosophy, but an organic evolution of existence, and ultimately you will learn this truth when you realize YOU ARE THE TREE!

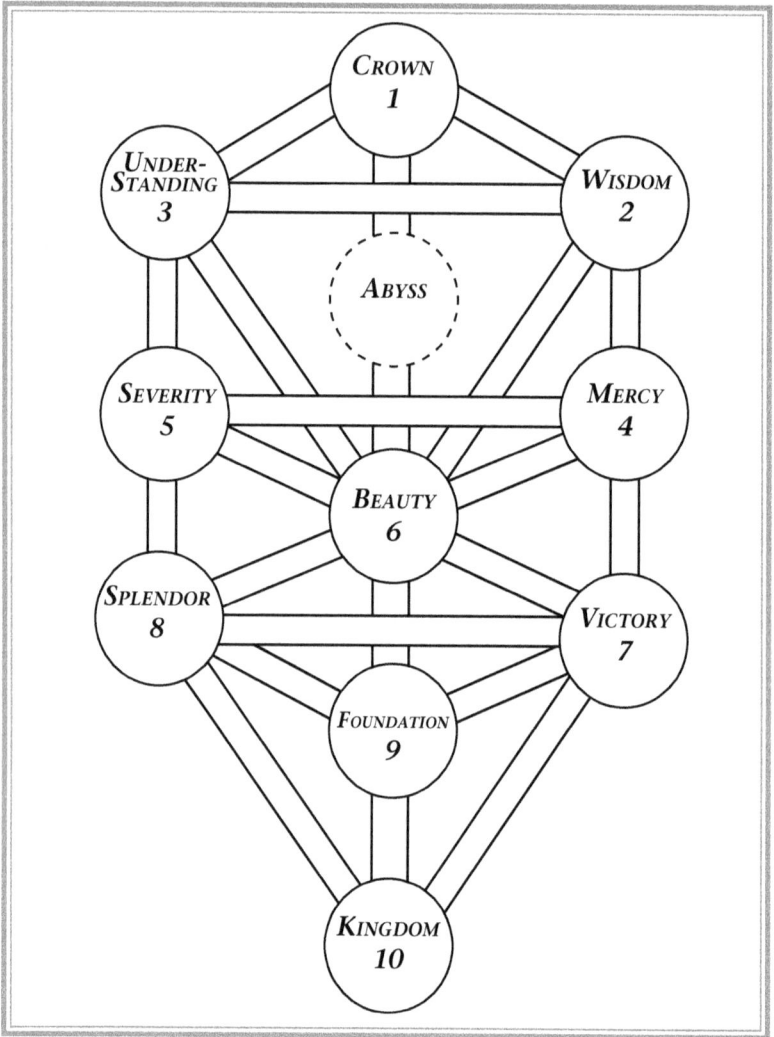

ILLUSTRATION 1. TREE OF LIFE MODEL

In this philosophical essay, the focus will be on a standard model of the Qabalistic tree. This model shows 10 Spheres and 22 Paths intersecting with the Spheres (Illustration 1). An additional sphere is depicted with dotted lines. It is the

Sphere of Great Mystery and noted as the Abyss. The Spheres are associated with the Creator and the Perfect Matrix of Source-Consciousness that is imprinted in every individual. The 22 paths (boughs on the tree) are the active flow of the Universe and the participation of each individual is called to express, live and gather the greater wisdom of the Perfect Matrix from these pathways. In fact, it is the responsibility of each individual to live and understand these qualities of consciousness.

The paths reveal how each person utilizes the gifts of their Purest Consciousness (Source) to experience and expand soul knowledge. Through personal experiences and awareness, one is led to the return of Oneness Consciousness—the Wisdom that you, the individual, are Source, and therefore, you are the Living Tree of Life.

Throughout this book, the Model is broken down into Triads. As you can see, Spheres 1, 2 and 3 are seen at the Highest point of the model. Their intersection by pathways forms a triangle. This is called the Supernal Triad, or, The Holy Trinity. Spheres 4, 5 and 6 are seen as the next Triad (inverted), and in Qabalistic theory, represents the Higher Self or Higher Consciousness of Humanity. It is also known as the Christ Conscious state or Avatar State of Consciousness. The triad that constitutes 7, 8 and 9 is considered the Triad of the Soul and its instinctive process to involute and evolve. Finally, another Triad is formed by the reconnection of 7 and 8 extending to the 10th Sphere. This is deemed the Vehicular Triad, acknowledging that the Universal State of Individuation manifests in the physical body or matter. The body, the vehicle of Source Light, explores the minute, as well as the most grand aspects of the Creator through this Triad. The Soul travels through matter within this vehicle. Exploration through experiences that occur life-after-life, provides greater insight to the Whole. These experiences are personal and explored through six levels of awareness known to be experienced as the following human conditions: Spiritual, Emotional, Mental, Physical, Ego and Soul (S.E.M.P.E.S.).

The Triads reveal the perfect model of Universal Consciousness as it releases Its Light and radiates greater, as well as lessor degrees of energy. Spinning vortices emit the Light of the Divine in specific states of consciousness and releases through the boughs (pathways) of the Tree. This provides a means for individuals to grasp and use Inner Source qualities. I will show how each person uses these qualities from positive modes as well as challenging modes. The challenges are simply the methods of awakening sleeping minds and hearts of the individual. Life challenges provide the desire to make changes and advance to the next levels of maturity. The positive activities are the reflection of the growth that flowers out of the challenge. From growth comes new and inviting experiences that open the gates of consciousness to weave awareness of the Whole that is existing in All. Through this process, awareness, self-actualization, and self-realization occurs.

Awareness provides the link to knowing what is happening in one's mind, heart and spirit, allowing for discernment to take place for right changes to self-actualize. In Self-Actualization, one awakens to her full potential and opportunities to live the gratifying life of soul fulfilment. Self-Realization provides wholeness-awareness, and therefore, recognition that the individual is indeed identical with the Divine Creator. Recognizing the power of the Living Tree within helps each person accomplish the achievement of these stages.

This written material will be done as simply as possible.

I will keep the information written in English and without the annotation of the Hebrew language (which often is the source of understanding the Tree of Life Philosophy). It will not be a deep and intellectual study. Texts and educational systems exist that go into depth meaning of Qabalah. It is my hope to bring you insight that you can grasp easily and then effortlessly note how you are the Living Tree. With the simplest of insights, you will be able to prune your tree, cultivate its growth, recognize its vibrant living qualities, and reap the rewards of its fruit.

To better assist your mind, emotions and inner knowing to integrate and emerge with a higher wisdom, a coloring project is suggested. Illustration 2 is a blank symbol of the traditional Tree of Life. I encourage you to make notations in the Spheres and Pathways, and color along as you go through the unfolding of information about each Triad. I will provide colors, words, and phrases you can write in the model to help you remain connected to the flow of wisdom and insight. The colors are the traditional hues provided through the World of Creation that holds the Matrix of Source Intent.

Enjoy your journey. Climb down the Tree and discover the Union of Source that exists within you and is you.

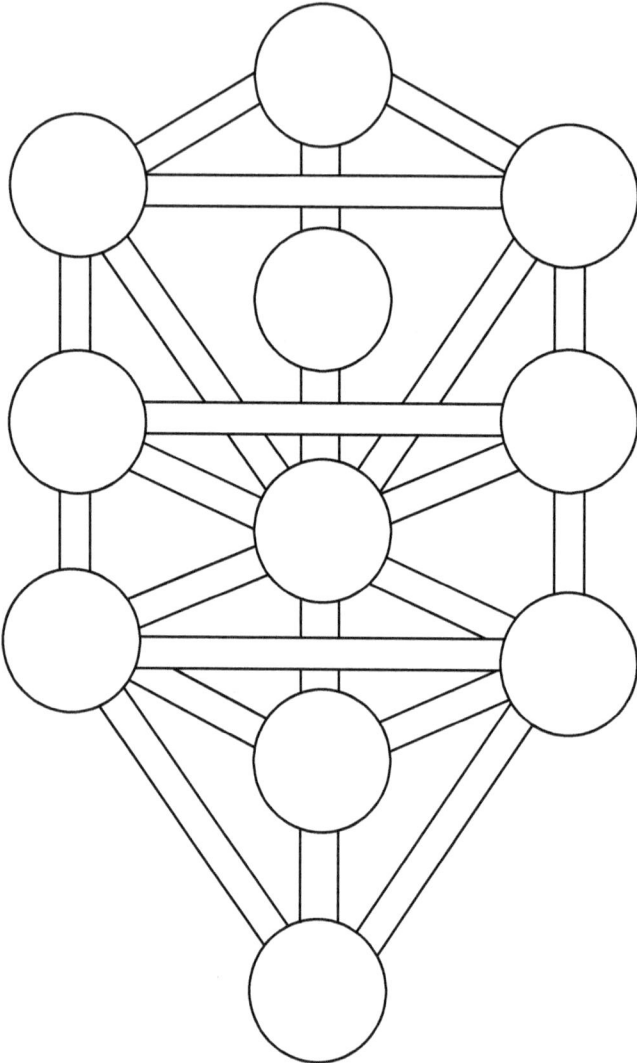

ILLUSTRATION 2. TREE OF LIFE TO COLOR

Part I

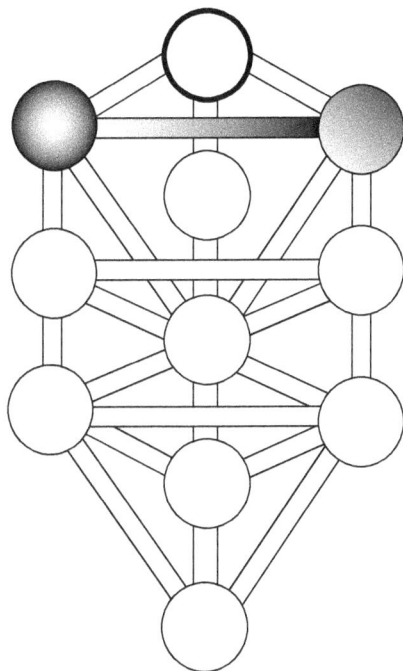

The Supernal Triad

Details to Reference

We are not ready to delve into the process of cultivating your tree until a few details are provided. You will find it useful to know about the Pillars of Consciousness, the Four Worlds of Expression, and the initiating qualities of Source, before starting out on the cultivation of your Living Tree awareness.

PILLARS OF CONSCIOUSNESS AND FLOW

Three Pillars of Consciousness and Flow are recognized within the symbolic tree, as noted below.

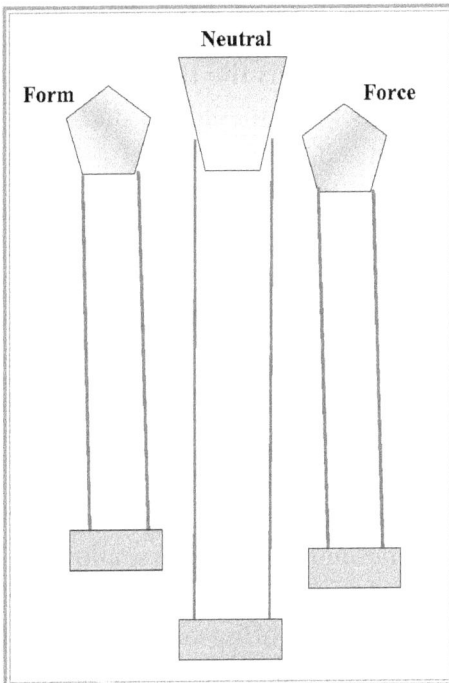

ILLUSTRATION 3. PILLARS OF THE LIVING TREE

As in the symbolic reality of all mystical wisdom, Pillars reveal stabilizing energy that hold things together as well. In fact, you need two pillars to create a balance and a support. Another understanding of the pillars is the power of a Paradox of the Universe—Polarities. Positive and Negative Charges of life. Things that attract and repel. Qualities of experiencing light and shadow, active and passive qualities, building things up and tearing things down, rewards and challenges, duality personified.

In the Tree of Life correspondences, three pillars are seen and create a balance for life experiences. Reference Illustrations 1 and 3 together. You will recognize that Spheres 2, 4, and 7 correspond with the Pillar of Force. Spheres 3, 5, and 8 correspond with the Pillar of Form, and the Spheres 1, 6, 9 and 10 reveal the Neutral Pillar. The Pillar of Force is masculine, active and thrusting energy. The Pillar of Form is feminine, receptive and contains the thrust of energy it receives. The Neutral Pillar is both masculine and feminine energy integrated, harmonized, and the focal point of each Triad (Spheres 1, 6, 9 and 10). The focal points use the Middle Pillar to produce the manifest power by way of the integration of Force and Form.

The Pillar of Force provides the emission of Source's Power and the release of the Seed of Life to be spread and multiply. It is constantly creating a myriad of expressions, that if not contained, simply maneuver through the chaotic cosmos, unused in the realm of matter.

The Pillar of Form provides the container of Source's Power that identifies and individuates, allowing the creative process to be transformed and used for specific experiences. This Pillar is necessary to bring order and define the seeds of existence. This pillar accepts the energy from the Pillar of Force. Without Force, the creative powers would remain held in storage. These desires, eggs of life, may lay dormant for aeons, locked away in a memory bank of the Universe. Force and Form are necessary to encourage the movement and structure of the Universal Conscious intent to manifest.

The Neutral Power refines the creation, stabilizes it and then harmonizes the final outcome. It tempers the Divine Design and releases it into the realm of matter. It liberates the Power of Higher Intent. You can say it is like the moment of an artist's review when the picture or sculpture looks perfect and is ready to be revealed to others. It is the moment when the musician realizes the music is ready to be played or sung, or the storyteller realizes the story is ready to be written or spoken. The perfect moment for manifestation occurs at the neutral point.

These pillars of consciousness are constantly moving through our inner self and manifested in our personal reality. Force creates urges, drives and desire. Form opens our consciousness to opportunities to create from our imagination and develop our drives and desires into a picture of reality. The power of neutrality provides the stage of balance to perform outcomes of the dreams imagined, designed, created and structured for use.

THE FOUR WORLDS

In all of my studies, whether Qabalistic, Celtic, Native American, or other Indigenous philosophies, there is always a story of four worlds with specific activities of the Universal Plan. Of course, in maintaining a connection to the Tree of Life philosophy for this book, I use the theory of the Four

Worlds as presented through the studies provided by The Builders of the Adytum. (This is a mystery school that teaches the philosophy of the Tree of Life.) It is through these worlds that we review the Universal Consciousness in evolution, moving from non-matter to matter.

The Four Worlds consist of:

The World of Origination
+ Inspiration
+ Initiation
+ Element of Fire
+ Realm of Pure Spirit

The World of Creation
+ Creative Imagination
+ Intuition/Emotions
+ Dreams
+ Element of Water
+ Realm of Archangels

The World of Formulation (+/-)
+ Focus/No Focus
+ Mental Acuity/Distraction
+ Decision/Indecision
+ Element of Air
+ Realm of the Order of Angels

The World of Manifestation
+ Completion
+ Materialization
+ Achievement
+ Element of Earth
+ Realm of the Divine Human

These realms of consciousness can also be recognized as used by our individual needs and desires. We are inspired to achieve great things through educational urges, a career drive, an important and loving relationship in our lives, a manifestation of a home, vehicle, etc.. From the original desire, we set out to create the ways and means to accomplish the inspired desire.

Our feelings rise in excitement and our dreams begin to take shape in our imagination. Our mind begins to release creative ideas, and we set about formulating the ways and means to obtain our outcome. Interestingly, as you will note, the World of Formulation holds a Divine Secret that we as humans have been uncovering through the agency of Psychology and Meta-psychology. We have a plus or minus scheme in this realm (a reward or challenge). We can use our ability to focus, make right decisions, communicate with the right individuals and set a strong intention to achieve our desire. Or, we can get caught up in the unconscious realms of fears, unworthiness, and beliefs that carry the "I can't" messages.

If we choose the challenge, we distort or abort the inspiration and deep desires to manifest. The distortion will be a minuscule manifest of the dream. We may start our education, but not finish it. We may enter a job, but not fulfill our dreams of a career. We will find ourselves locked out of the Abundance Bank, and struggle with the odds and ends of minor manifestations. If in the power of a full abortion, we simply will not see a manifest of our desire. Nothing happens. No desires fulfilled. Disappointment resides in our mental and emotional states of consciousness. Yes, this realm of consciousness asks us to be alert, awake and aware so we may take charge of our inner consciousness that holds old maladjustive attitudes and beliefs, and change them to empowered knowing.

Once we create a Higher Intent, flow through the worlds in their most empowered state of consciousness, we enter the realm of Manifestation with a delight in life. We experience a fully activated manifestation of whatever our original inspiration stirred, and an ability to utilize the gift of materialization until we are complete and ready to start on a new process of inspired desires. We see and live what our inspiration and desire initiated. We feel the success of completion and fulfillment of a dream. We feel confident and courageous enough to take new steps and accept new risks to create again. We know we can create an outcome that is the product of our desires.

As we head into the awareness of being the Living Tree of Life, I urge you to take a few minutes and contemplate something that you *really, really, really* want to manifest in your world. Write about it in a journal. Fully allow yourself to feel it. Visualize it with color, action, positive intent and knowing the absolute outcome. Notice if any fears, judgements or disbeliefs surface. If they do, remind yourself that all of these aspects are part of past experiences that are now done and complete. You do not have to let them take control of you now. Most certainly, you have the empowered state of your Higher Self that you can choose to align with and overcome all shadows of maladjustments that you may have used, up until now.

Empower yourself and know (feel, believe and allow) you are in a new state of creativity and you are going to use a formula of Source that is embedded within your deep inner psyche through the Tree of Life matrix. Make the choice to take charge right now and act on this choice. As you work with the process of being aware of the power of the Living Tree, you will discover that you are aligned with the ability to create and manifest as you follow the spheres and pathways described in this work. As you flow with this written work, you will be using the Energy of Source and flowing through polarities (Force and Form), creating through the Worlds, and manifesting through the neutral pillar. Enjoy creating as the One Great Mind created the existence you now know as yourself and the world.

Using the flow of the Four Worlds, we can also connect with Timing (see Illustration 4). Though this is not an exact timing, it most certainly comes close. If we are inspired by Spirit, this flow of consciousness must move from a deep inner level of our psyche.

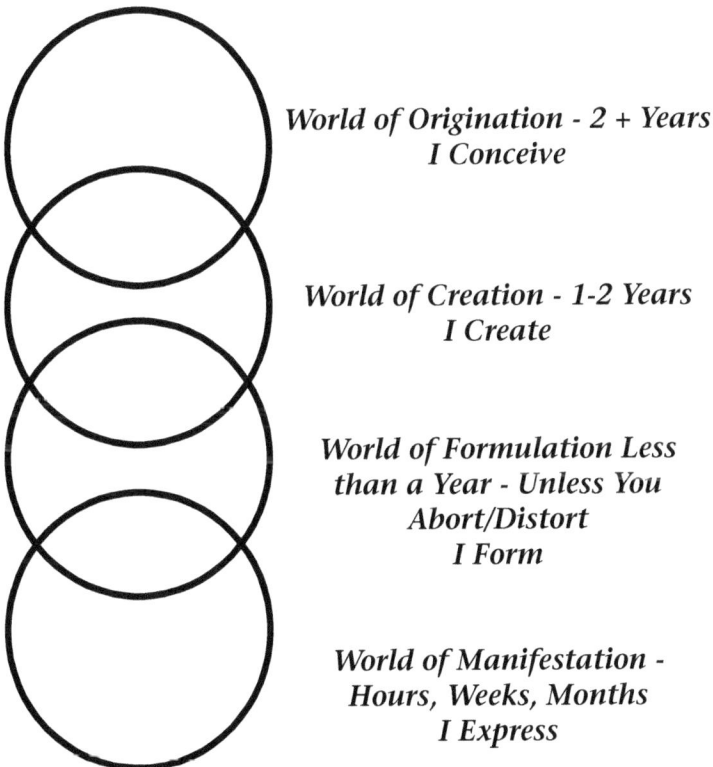

World of Origination - 2 + Years
I Conceive

World of Creation - 1-2 Years
I Create

World of Formulation Less than a Year - Unless You Abort/Distort
I Form

World of Manifestation - Hours, Weeks, Months
I Express

ILLUSTRATION 4. TIMING THROUGH THE WORLDS OF CONSCIOUSNESS

Often this inspiration gives us an excitement but we realize we are in no way ready to put the desire into action. It will take some time (two years or more) to develop the outcome. For instance, many years ago I was working out at a local gym. Aerobic dance was the craze of the time. I loved it. The anaerobic exercises right after the dancing were great for strength building and stretching. However, I felt the instructor was doing the movements incorrectly, which could injure me or other members of the class. I sat in a sauna after class, thinking about the situation and felt an inspiration move through me. It came through a thought-form.

First of all, the thought indicated that if I was going to be so judgmental, then I should do something about this myself. Next, I imagined myself instructing others. I went from the sauna to the hot tub where I could see through a window. I watched the next class of students dance, twist their bodies, and relax. At that point, my dream-vision got a bit stronger. Truth be known, I had no way to realize what it would take to become an instructor, much less open a business. I had been given an "Original" idea. I said to this thought-form, which I had taken to be in Inspiration from God, "I will do this. Guide me." Guidance occurred.

I began to devour professional information about exercise, specifically aerobic dance. I found an Exercise Physiology Class and through an organization, took certification classes at UCSD. Before long, I was offering classes in the corporate world. Two years later, I was opening my own aerobic dance studio. It was quite a lesson of Inspiration-to-Manifestation. Deep desire, delight in the process, and a strong intention to learn, as well as serve humanity, kept my vision going and the outcome developing. The love of dancing emerged in the art form of aerobic fitness programs. The love of caring for others emerged into the programs of health and fitness.

If you are already in the knowing of what you **really, really, really** want, then you have likely passed the essence of Origination. You may be working from the Creative World. If so, you are using your inner desire and are day dreaming, using creative imagination, and perhaps drawing out the way and means to achieve your manifest.

Are you past the Creative world and into the World of Formulation? If you are, take care to be alert and awake to any thoughts or feelings that might undermine your deep and purposeful desire. Remember, you are at the point of formulating and fully structuring your desire, or distorting and possibly aborting the fulfillment of your purpose. Stay focused. Be deliberate in your formulation. Remain clear and release anything that seems to be in the way of your final manifest. No thing, person or event can get in your way unless you allow it to be so. Take charge! Be ready to manifest.

Before the Beginning

No Thing - Ring Cosmos

No Limit - Ring Chaos

No Limit to Light - Ring Pass Not

Pure Source has no beginning and no end. However, it has stations of consciousness where something occurs and an outburst of individual qualities manifests into awareness. In Qabalistic lore, before the matrix of the Tree of Life was conceived, the essence of Source remained in a state of unidentifiable substance and No Thing existed. From the No Thing, an initiation of energy activated Every Thing in the Ring Cosmos. The swirl of unfathomable magnitude sent a vibrational arc of energy stirring the Power of No Limit and the essence of creative personification of infinity initiated the power of Ring Chaos (creative outbursts).

As the chaos released through creative expression from the dream within the Mind of Source, the firmament released the power of Unlimited Light. This energy activated and initiated the vibrant expression of Ring Pass Not. The containment of infinite energy, through this combined vibration, reveals the presentation of angels, galaxies, stars, planets, mineral, plants, animals, humans, and all creatures of the Unlimited Universe. The impact of these three qualities of Supernal Consciousness is what contains, creates and purely expresses as All Things and is recognized as the holder and expression of the Universal Living Tree of Life (see Illustration 5).

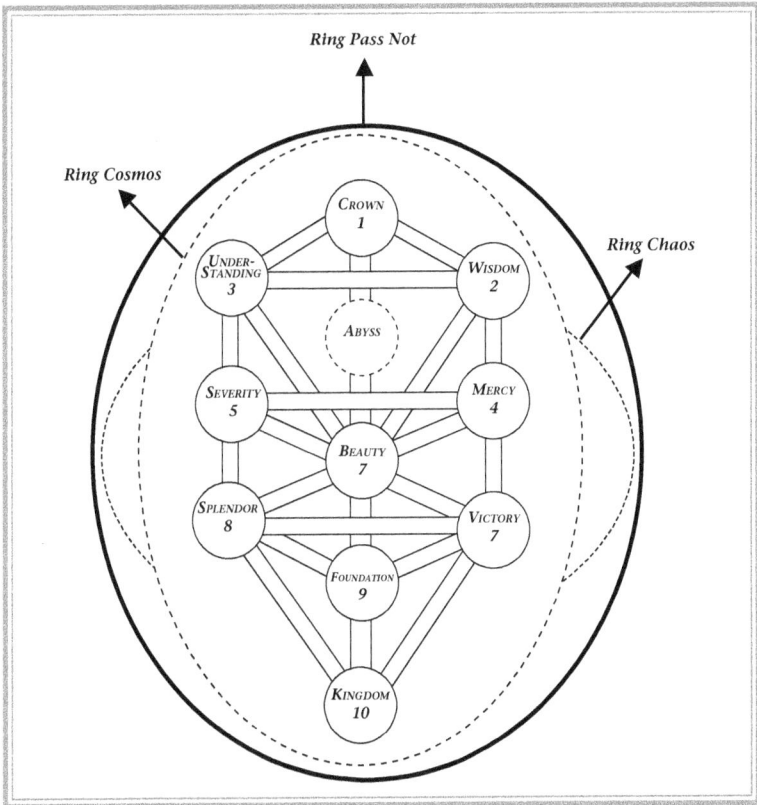

ILLUSTRATION 5. TREE IN THE CIRCLES OF SOURCE

THE PARADOX

A paradox reveals that something that is, or appears to be, contradictory is, in fact, true. From a Universal standpoint, in this discussion, there are three paradoxes we review when learning about the Living Tree of Life we know as Source:

◆ The Universe is Nothing and is Everything

◆ The Universe is neither masculine nor feminine and is masculine and feminine

◆ The Universe is Oneness and every living creature is the Universe

The premise that exudes from these points most certainly reveals the knowledge that we are One, are neither masculine nor feminine, yet both, and we are Nothing yet Everything. We are Source. As Source, we are the Living Tree of Life. We are the seed, the trunk, the branches, the leaves, flowers and fruit. With that being a premise of Truth, then it is to be celebrated. How do we celebrate this wisdom? By being cognitive, creative and expressive as the Living Tree, which is constantly moving through seasons of life, death and rebirth: manifesting, changing and manifesting new states of existence.

From the Tree of Life, a doctrine is formed: A Sacred Book of Wisdom. The study called Qabalah is an interpretation of the Secret Doctrine or Book of Life. It is known that you can study the doctrine through meditation and internal connection with Source. Deep meditation, ritualistic meditation, and willingness to go beyond the Logic of the 3rd Dimension are needed to truly understand the Tree of Life. Studies in books help confirm what you learn, but remember that all books and all teachers of The Tree of Life have "translated" the wisdom gleaned from the deeper resources of meditation. My encouragement to you is to not only read this book, but meditate, contemplate, feel and live the knowledge of the Tree of Life. Do not just read. This will keep you in 3rd dimensional intellect and you will miss the Greater Truth. Get into the Heart Beat of the Wisdom of the Universal Tree through your meditations.

THE TREE OF LIFE IS A SYMBOL OF CONSCIOUSNESS IN MOTION

✦ Your journey begins with the intellect, moves to inner awareness and ends with Knowing.

- You cannot Intellectualize Source

- You can only **KNOW** Source

- When you **Know** Source, you become gods and goddesses (Light Beings: Humans vibrating at a higher order of energy awareness)

  - Do not get lost in Intellect

  - Move with Desire *and* Intellect and experience Source (The Living Tree of Life) through prayer, meditation, contemplation and feeling

  - It is only in this manner that you will "contain" the vast energy of Source and Know!

✦ Unseen realities of the Universe must be translated into a language usable by the Intelligence of the Human thinking process.

- The Language of God/Goddess is presented to humanity as symbolism

- Symbolism is the manner in which humanity attempts to explain God/Goddess.

- Symbolism is the Common Language that exists for explaining the Seen and Unseen.

- The Tree of Life is a symbolic messenger of the meaning of Oneness

The following pages present a simple understanding and yet, a profound use of your consciousness to recognize the Living Tree that you are, and thus, the Creator that you are. May you find that you are able to initiate a desire into a manifested reality by reading and consuming the fruit of this wisdom presented to you. Even if you have studied the Tree of Life before, become like the innocent and curious novice. Enter the study of this wisdom with a fresh and open consciousness and deep feelings of wanting to recognize your empowered state: A Creator of your reality, a Manifestor of your reality, and a Master of your reality .

Enjoy the journey and create!

The Supernal Triad and Pathways

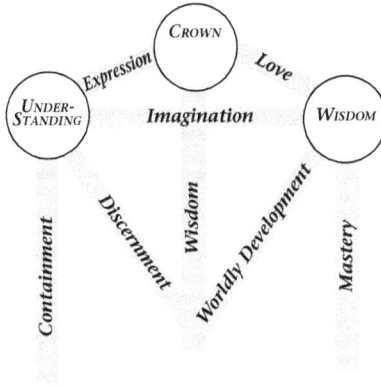

Now, we enter the conscious review of the tree and begin to climb down from the top, which is the Point of Origination. We begin with the Supernal Triad and connect with its flow of energy.

The Supernal Triad (Triangle) is also called The Supreme Mysteries and The Holy Trinity. It consists of three vortices representing states of Source and the rays of light flowing through all existence.   As the vortices exude rays of light, they release and simplify the Primal Source for use by individual states of consciousness. This simplification is recognizable in the pathways of the matrix. The vibrant masses of whirling light of the Holy Trinity are identified as:

♦ Crown: The Un-namable Supreme
Being of All Life
Deemed: Almighty Principle

+ Wisdom: Divine Father Principle, most
frequently known as God
Deemed: Direction and Active
Energy of Evolution

+ Understanding: Divine Feminine Principle,
most frequently known as Goddess.
Deemed: Universal Womb. Memory
and Genetic Coding (RNA/DNA)

The rays of light, seen as pathways, emit unconditional love, expression of Divine Mind, creative imagination, worldly development, mastery of life, containment of universal energy, and the power to discern. Much more comes through these emanations, as you will see. Most certainly the vital and succulent resources of the Fruit of Life.

SPHERE 1 – THE CROWN

The Primal Source emanates from a swirling mass. It is called "I AM" and is the focal point of the entire matrix of the Tree of Life. More specifically, it is the Focal Point of the Supernal Triad and the Whole Tree of Life   It initiates Existence of All Existence. Its movement causes such a jolt it is deemed a lightening flash and the "big bang" that releases the Intention of Source Consciousness to exist in multi-expressions recognizable by individuating.

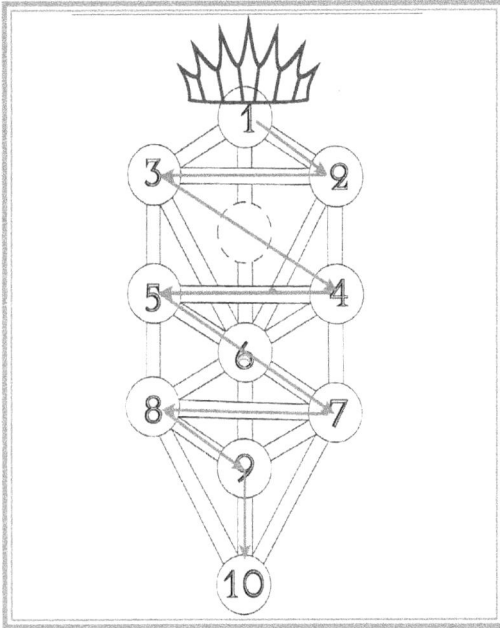

ILLUSTRATION 6. THE LIGHTNING FLASH

As the liberating burst of life exudes from this point of reference, the Law of Correspondences is unleashed. At the very moment, the power of That Which is Above, is That Which is Below and That which is Below is That Which is Above, expresses the Oneness of Everything. In less than a blink of an eye, you are Source and Source is you. In less than the blink of an eye, No Thing becomes recognizable as Everything in Existence, and all things correspond to all other things.

Remember the edict to know what you *really, really, really* want? It is at this point, the First Sphere of Consciousness, that you need to know the Inspiration of your desire has been ignited. You are the caretaker of the seed of this desire and you can follow the lightening path throughout this book as reference to the birthing and manifesting what you *really,*

really, really want. Dream, imagine and feel the desire, but also note: Nothing needs to be left in the dreaming mind. Now the desire can flow and evolve into a manifested state, just as all existence manifested at the point of the Flash and Big Bang of Universal Consciousness.

The Crown is the Focus of this triad and provides the energy of Force (Essence) and Form (Containment) in the neutral, sculptured and refined quality of Source Consciousness. Brilliant Light releases the power of Source. In fact, at the Crown level of Illustration 2, you can color a brilliant white light (add white glitter to reveal this sphere's activity). Releasing this Light in your consciousness is a guiding force that reminds you to return to awareness of your Oneness. You utilize this brilliance to Know Wholeness and Wholeness utilizes this Brilliance to express your desires.

Take some time to meditate on your oneness and you may hear the Sphere of Light vibrating a holy tune that reminds you that You and Source are One Alignment with the same intent: to manifest your desire. Allow yourself to feel the One Intention and the powerful surge of swirling energy that is "Will-Filled" to manifest.

The most powerful angel, Archangel Metatron, oversees this sphere and assists you in remembering the power within you, the Divine aspect that you are. Metatron helps you hold the matrix of your desire with reverence and love. He will help you remember that you are the Divine Essence manifesting everything through the agency of a single light: your soul, exuding the light and plans of this lifetime.

Encouraging energy moves through this sphere of consciousness. It is the encouragement to Be. It spurs the evolution of individuation into existence. Please note that existence is not just human beings. It is the existence of Everything. Your dream is a part of the Everything and your desire is the "readiness of Source" to express the dream into matter through the agent of light deemed you! Do not be shy. Feel the Presence of Intent and follow through with your goal to bring what you *really, really, really* want into your world of experiences.

From this Sphere, Crown, rays of light emanate. They are three Pathways: Love, Expression and Wisdom. They are the pathways that release the power of the vortex of Crown and provide an ease for you to utilize the energy of the Supernal Focus of Consciousness within the Holy Trinity. The Ray of Will and Power, as well as the Ray of Regeneration and Trans-formation initiate the vibration of the three pathways.

Source has only one point of reference and is One Dimen-sional. This simply means Source holds Its perfect Intent to do Its Great Work. It intends to Manifest all Existence into a form that is recognizable and useable. It does not sway from this intent and envelops the intent with Unconditional Love, the Will to Express and the Power to reveal Wisdom. The Will to Evolve is released through the focal point of the Supernal Triad, and you can take the responsibility for the evolution by remaining intentful in manifesting your desire by remaining focused on your perfect desire to express the Great Work in the individuated quality of your desire.

PATH OF LOVE

This is the bough on the Tree of Life that ignites the Elec-tric Fire-Light of Source within Individual States of Being. Its color is a faint yellow – so soft it is nearly white. Color that path on Illustration 2.

This path is the freedom and initiating of soul-seeds of expressions of the Universe. It is a cultivating energy providing developing powers to foster the growth of an idea and desire. It is an energy within you that knows you have Free Will and Choice and are always held in the Loving Embrace of Source.

Embedded within this path is the Law of Love. This is Sacred Law. It represents the true nature of the Universe. It encompasses all forms of existence, is non-judgmental, constant, perfect and unchangeable. It asks that you hold all life sacred and come from a space of love when dealing with the myriad of aspects of your existence. Know how to use this Law in a state of empowerment.

✦ Feel the Power of Unconditional Love within you and Live this power

✦ See Everything from the Eyes of Source

✦ See your desire as perfect in the Eyes of Source

✦ See perfect qualities of yourself and others for all are Divine Light

Know the virtue of this path of love is your ability to Trust the power within you, be free of judgment and free from concerns of what can begin and what must end. Just be. In that way, you are spontaneous and release the ability to manifest your desire through a timeless space and a formless form of existence.

The challenges and vices on this path can create distrust, fear and the living in states of airy-fairy illusion. It is the initiation of separation and polarity existence, causing unconscious levels to believe in "less than" realities. In the challenge of this path, love may be fleeting. Your free will may be recognized as the will to live limited and uncomfortable realities, feeling unloved and lacking creativity. At such states of existence, you will have to conform to the following processes to uncover True Source within you and the freedom to follow this path with its ultimate positive field of awareness.

✦ Recognize the perfection of Human Life is its imperfection

✦ See the incredible qualities that others are revealing to you and about:

- Reflecting You through their actions

- Teaching You

- Challenging You

- Supporting You

- Revealing unconditional and conditional love

✦ Use the power of compassionate detachment

- Do not take things personally; everything has a purpose in your life

- Allow yourself to individually experience the events of your life

- Be an observer of life and create after you observe what you can fashion from your dreams and desires

- Do not remain stuck in the belief of separation by allowing yourself to know that the initiation of polarities stimulates the power to create material qualities of the Divine Design held in the Mind of Source

- Live unconditional love no matter what "appearance" of no love seems to grasp your imagination

Once you open to the path of Love and exude your freedom to manifest, then you will be supporting the power of the 1st Sphere of Consciousness, the Crown. A secret resides here for you to manifest what you really want: it calls for you to Love the Desire unconditionally. It calls for you to love it deeply and to keep a singular intent to manifest through the action of love.

From this path, the Initiation of the Pillar of Force occurs. On this path the release of the power of the next sphere, Wisdom, is activated. However, before connecting to the Sphere of Wisdom, connect with the Rays of Light emanating from the other paths that are radiating from the I AM center of the 1st sphere.

PATH OF EXPRESSION

This path is soft yellow in color. This bough of the tree is a slightly brighter yellow than the Path of Love, but not a brilliant yellow. Color it into your Tree of Life in Illustration 2. I also hope you are adding a word or phrase into the pathways you are connecting with as well.

From the very word, Expression, we gain a hint that the Greater Source has an intention to Express Itself. So it is within ourselves. There is an intention to express and cause characteristics of life to denote special qualities. In fact, this path calls forth the Power of Word, the gift of Sound that emanates the vibration of formlessness to form, similar to the message about the Divine as noted in the *Bible:* And God said, "Let there be light; and there was light." The Logos, or Word of God, brought forth existence of material qualities of the One Essence, God Itself.

Expression is not just words, it is a manifested quality. To express this book, I had to think about it, speak about it, write it and have it published. As a published work, it reveals the expression through solid matter recognizable as pages with letters, and a binding with a colorful expression that stirs the interest of readers.   As Source thought Itself, it released Its Sound and published Its results as individuated states of All Existence. This attracted the colorful expression of All:

- ✦ Human Beings of many colors
- ✦ Blue day sky and black night sky
- ✦ Rainbows
- ✦ Planets of many colors
- ✦ And the list goes on

You have already expressed what you really want, and on this path, you will put sound to this expression. Affirm, out loud to your Source Consciousness, the power of Love you carry and the desire to achieve the full manifest of your dream.

From this path, the Law of Expression is released. This Law reveals:

- ✦ The Divine is in constant expression through all living things
- ✦ Expression is the power of Source creating, manifesting and delivering the meaning of all life

- ✦ It is an encoded empowerment within all living creatures to demonstrate and identify itself through its expression

- ✦ Whether through thought, word or deed, an expression is always occurring

Expression is a form of Magic

- ✦ Sounds create a vibration, which in turn, creates a manifestation

- ✦ Words create a reality

- ✦ Tone and timbre creates an action or re-action

- ✦ You are heard and defined by your words, tone and timbre

- ✦ You define by your words, tone and timbre

- ✦ You define energy of Source by your words, tone and timbre

Know what are you creating with your words, tone and timbre. Is it what you want? Make sure your words carry the tone and timber of positive alignment with your desires.

The Pathway of Expression provides a conduit for the Messages and Messengers of the Universe to flow through you. It is a channel in which the Energy of Source Vibrates and prepares to enter the Holy Living Temple (individuated aspects of Source), manifesting as a variety of qualities. It allows undifferentiated energy to come to a focal point and manifest. You activate the qualities of this path by living the virtue of clear site, focus and intent.

You may set vibrations into chaos and an inability to manifest through the vice of loss of intent and focus. You then disable your inner intent. In fact, review other times in your life when you wanted to manifest something you felt was important to you, but you lacked focus, did not hold your intent, and fell into illusionary expressions. You know you did not hold the conduit of expression in a way that allowed your manifest to occur. In fact, you likely spoke positively of the desire and then immediately added statements such as, "if I only can," or, "I hope nothing gets in my way," or "if I only have time."

On the other hand, remember times in your life when you did manifest a desire. You felt intentful, kept your focus, and continually expressed your desire. You spoke of it with conviction. You were willing to go from beginning to end without loss of your intention. So it was, you manifested. So it is a From Above (Origination) to Below (Manifestation) you maintained an expression of purpose.

It is through this pathway that you may "hear" the voices of messengers ignite an inspiration, offer a thought to contemplate, and engage in soul-communication with you. It is from this path that you are gifted the power to "see" what is before you and activate your clairvoyant abilities. (This is the power to see what is, before it is.)

Through the path of Expression, Source transforms energy from an idea into a formula to be manifested as It activates the next Sphere, Understanding. Again, we will review this sphere after moving through an awareness of the next light emanating from the 1st Sphere and the I AM Center of all existence. It is the Path of Wisdom and radiates in a soft blue color.

PATH OF WISDOM

This path is the conductor of Universal Intelligence. It creates a conduit for the Mind of Source to Individuate through both an Unconscious Channel and through the Conscious Channel of Individuation. The unconscious channel provides the foundation for Universal Intention to be manifested and incorporated in all Laws of the Universe. The Laws are automatically set into motion with full wisdom for their use. The Intelligence of Source is encoded in all Laws and are decoded by each individual response and action.

The consciousness of individuals, therefore, has automatic connection to the Universal Intention and Universal Laws, and utilizes them whether aware of them or not. When wisely using the laws, the power of positive expression occurs quite naturally. For instance, if you are aware of the Law of Cause and Effect, you can realize that in order to achieve what you want, you must initiate at the point of Cause. At this point, you lead with an intention to fully align with the higher wisdom to transport you through the stages of manifestation with the initial power of love. Then you open to expression, with an intent to remain focused on the outcome and disassociated from all fear, lack and limitation. Cause calls you to hold the vision of your intent in a picture of perfect expression and design every step from the point of original thought to the final outcome by unfolding the vision as though every act you do is a weaving of color, light and presentation of the final design.

The unconscious use of the laws often is seen by an outcome that we "thought" we did not want. However, if we set out to manifest a desire, but place fear, doubt and belief that something or others can control the outcome, the causal moment carries the misdirected manifest – we have created unconsciously. Then, we see an outcome that is not what we want. All Laws are automatic and neutral. Whatever we throw into the mix of thought and feeling, will automatically create and honor what we placed within the blend. No judgment, simply allowing what is created to be.

The secret powers of this pathway is the gift of uniting the individual with the consciousness of Source. The secret reveals that there is a constant, conductive force through this pathway that releases the Power of Source and its immeasurable wisdom into individual qualities. This allows you to know that you are never without the wisdom you need to express and manifest anything you desire.

The Law of Wisdom on this pathway helps you use the power of this conductive and unifying path. It calls for the knowledge and right use of polarities. It is the first state of consciousness released on the Neutral Pillar. This Law intimates duality and the power of two opposed aspects as teachers of knowledge which, when understood, combine into a coherent Whole.

Leaving the point of Crown on the Tree of Life, the Duality process occurs through the spheres of Wisdom and Understanding. Synthesization, through the path of wisdom, is originated and activated through the Universe. We recognize this in the expressions of:

- ✦ Light - Dark
- ✦ Living - Non Living
- ✦ Peace - War
- ✦ Truth - Lie
- ✦ Conscious - Unconscious
- ✦ Non Matter - Matter

- ✦ Warm - Cold
- ✦ Active - Passive
- ✦ Fertile - Non fertile

All of these states of duality are used to initiate, manifest, explore, experience, and complete cycles of universal expression.

How do you use the Law of Wisdom? You utilize your power to synthesize polarities and dualities so you will know what is necessary to manifest your desires. You may activate the empowered use of this law via:

- ✦ Supplicating Prayer (asking for assistance to use your higher wisdom)
- ✦ Meditation to gain access to higher consciousness
- ✦ Dreaming to gain access to your inner consciousness and decipher what is going on at your subconscious level (clearing obstacles of fear and false beliefs)
- ✦ Intuition
- ✦ Educating
  - • Schools (of all types)
  - • Reading
  - • Listening to Masters
- ✦ Living with awareness
- ✦ Understanding and synthesizing what you learn
- ✦ Using your wisdom

The three pathways from the Sphere named Crown activate your power to know how important it is to Love, Express and use your Wisdom when you initiate a desire for an outcome to be manifested. As we travel through the next sphere of light, further qualities of the universe will reveal the power you have within yourself to continue to evolve the manifestation of your desire.

SPHERE 2—WISDOM

This sphere reveals the rotation of the Wheel of Life as the Supernal Consciousness releases Itself from a Single Point of Unlimited Light into the realms if individualization, and thus Limited Light. The statement of Limited Light does not mean "less than," but rather provides a means to identify the multiple-aspects of Source.

It is here that the Cosmic field of energy is swirling and projecting Itself. Through the prism of Brilliant Light, the first containment is forced into existence, and yet it is still not contained. An oxymoron? Yes. Multi-facets of Source are spinning and ejecting a climatic force through a Cosmic Net of Ring Chaos. It is here that we engage in the defining words of the Divine Masculine Principle: Aba, Father, God.

Pure Spirit, through Its unconditional love, activates and excites a prolonged lengthening of t ime and space, anti-matter and matter, releasing a Primary Expression from which all others will develop through this vortex called Wisdom. The Life-Force set forward the power of Duplication and Reflection, duplicating itself and causing all individuated aspects to reflect the Face of Source and see the Face of Source in All Things, especially itself.

This sphere is the crown of the Pillar of Force, also called the Pillar of Mercy. It is active, projecting, and compelling life To Be. In the swirling, projecting powers, creative chaos reigns. Spinning and spiraling, cycling and clashing. The cells of life instigate powers of development through colliding ideas, and master-mind ideals. This creative chaos is the point of consciousness that reveals every thing that Is, Is to Be and Will Become. It is the Past, Present and Future swirling and diving, undulating and expelling itself. It is the whirling forces that fashions the design of the Universe.

We learn in this sphere of consciousness that the Light and Dark, Heaven and Earth, Non-matter and Matter were initiated. We learn that the stars and planets, and the firmament took place in the scheme of creative, chaotic, infinite design. We also learn that this power is the power every one of us uses to create anything that we feel a desire to create.

Creative chaos is known by us through the influx and out flow of ideas that we simply find swimming through our thoughts and feelings. They agitate and do not form a structure of use. For a while, they must be here and be gone. They enter our feelings and exit through thinking, or vice versa. Ideas flow into visual design and de-materialize through other thoughts and colorful ideas. These are important moments of inspiration. They titillate our dreams and aspirations. They cause us to seek more and find ways to gather multi-faceted realities that will help formulate the desired creative idea.

In this Sphere of Consciousness, the Archangel Ratziel is called forward to release the knowledge of the Book of Life. Of course, it is the Wisdom of the Universal Mind. It is through his sacred holding of the Matrix of this Sphere of Consciousness that the emanation of the color Silver is released. Yes, color this sphere Silver on Illustration 2. It is the 2nd Sphere on the Tree of Life. Silver carries the gift of quickened intuitive powers that allow you to slip into and out of the Wisdom of the Universal Mind.

Archangel Ratziel is given charge over all the Records of

Life and Earthly existence. As one who Shows the Way, he guides through the Lights of the Stars and Planets, and thus rules the wisdom of Astrology and the secret that we are all guided by the light of the stars (just as the Magi were guided to the Christ Consciousness). In angelic lore, Ratziel is known to have written a Book of Angels and released the Book of Healing to Noah. He releases wisdom to those who request insight. This Angelic consciousness is most helpful when you are swirling through thoughts and finding the Light of Guidance to create the ultimate formula for the manifested outcome.

Your power of living this sphere on the Tree of Life is the chaos of creative thinking that stirs ideas for manifesting. It is also the sphere you use for guidance and wisdom that is revealed through free-forming thoughts and inspirations that help you instigate new outcomes in your life. You may wish to produce an idea into a project, but not know how. Your inner self guides you to this point of consciousness and many thoughts form and flow. Many ideas cycle and circle. Your mind may not grasp the insights completely, but the joy of creative urges keep you seeking. One idea overcomes another until the "right idea" configures and you set out to accomplish your goal. Perhaps it is not a product, but a ways and means to heal, or a power to form a union, or create a separation necessary to advance your growth. When you do not seem to have an answer, this is where your higher instinct will guide you so you can cycle through a thousand ideas to get to the one most important concept that will help you form a reality best suited for the outcome you desire.

Of course, there is a challenge that you experience in this sphere of consciousness when you do not take charge and know you are an empowered being. The challenge you live is the spinning and spiraling out of control mentally, emotionally and physically. The whirlwind of your life keeps you from the balance and harmony of your existence. You cannot find the light in the darkness of your disturbances. Chaos reigns with a negative vengeance of incomplete desires, lack of clarity, lack of direction and lack of fulfillment. Accumulation of clutter gets in your way. Wisdom is not used, only urgencies of immediate gratification, false entitlements and misuse of power.

The way out of the challenge is to seek the higher wisdom. Connect with one who Shows the Way, a Master of Chaos. Use the virtue of Devotion and remain devoted to Source, devoted to your desire, and devoted to a harmonious outcome. Then, the Creative Powers will ease you through the maze of designs you need to manage and materialize in your desired outcome.

The pathways from the Sphere of Wisdom are the Path of Imagination, the Path of Worldly Development, and the Path of Mastery. Each carry the creative chaos and the power of wisdom toward the goal of manifestation.

PATH OF IMAGINATION

This pathway is the conduit for the Law of Creative Imagination. From the Essence of Source, we see the Creative idea of Individuation as this path opens the doorway for the passage of souls into existence. The Creative desire of Source is to express in multiple arenas: animal, plant, mineral, humans, angels, stars, planets, galaxies, etc. The doorway of the imagination of Source, open and ready to contain and grow the cells of existence is now in a stage of involuting.

Embedded in each soul is the power to imagine, create and fulfill abundant realities of Source. The original and fertile idea of Source is released through this conduit of emerald green light. It is the station of consciousness that holds the Visible Light of Intelligence which emanates the awareness of the fundamental qualities of holiness and that which is concealed. When you are connected with this intelligence, there is nothing concealed and you are connected to the intent of Source to create.

The release of the Law of Creative Imagination imparts a gift of the gracefulness of Source. The Divinely given talents and blessings of each soul are released through this channel of light. That which is concealed may be revealed. You access these talents by the use of the Law of Creative Imagination. The power of creative imagination, provides the building blocks of all creation. It sets into order the dream, the wishful feelings and the desire. You must simply follow a trail of inspirational feelings, visual ideas and form a picture of the desired outcome. Through the formulation of the picture, you must maintain the positive feelings of belief and knowing that the imagined field of thinking is real. For it is at this point, the substance of the Universe is forming the building blocks to be called into an alliance with matter and therefore into the field of materialization. During the time of creative imaging, you must be sure your thoughts and emotions are congruent. They must be on the same wavelength of positive thinking and feeling or your outcome will be distorted or aborted.

I like to use the acronym of T.E.A. and T.E.A.M. when working with the power of Creative Imagination.

T = Thoughts, E = Emotions, A = Actions. I begin with this process first, realizing that my actions will depict the status of my thoughts and emotions and let me know if they are in congruent alignment or need adjustment. If I think and feel positively and have no lurking, unseen fears, then my actions will take me on the course necessary to realize my desire.

If I am fully on a positive course, then the acronym of T.E.A.M. will come into play with M = Manifestation. All four layers of consciousness are activated and the manifest will prove it. However, if my thoughts and emotions lack congruency, then my actions will take me off course. I will avoid opportunities, and feel the misguidance of being a victim of life when my manifestations are distorted or absolutely aborted. However, if all is on right course of positive realization, my manifest will be pure, clean and contain within it the emotions of joy and delight in life as I see the form of my ideals materialize.

Most certainly, to live the empowered point of this path, it is time for you to spend an hour or so in the mind-set of creative imagination. Take time to imagine and feel your desire from its beginning, right on through its materialization. Put color, people and needed events into your imagination. Pay attention to your T.E.A. Even in the point of imagination, your actions can begin to distort or abort the desired outcome, especially if your thoughts are running on the joy and greatness of the vision, but your emotions are flowing over the fears, phobias and all the reasons why you cannot have what you want. Your actions will distort time, and encourage urgencies to leave your meditation and your imagination will run pictures of false realities becoming real. If you find yourself in the challenge, release your fears and set out again in the power of Faith that you and Source carry the same intention: to manifest your desires. Return to your creative imagination process.

This path on the Tree of Life is the State of Conscious of the Divine as it creates galaxies, worlds, humans, animals, plants and minerals and more that we cannot see and do not know of, yet

+ All souls are encoded with the power of Creative Imagination and the ability to build their experiences through creative-imaging that stirs the power of manifestation.

+ Humanity uses this law to co-create.

  • It is humanity's most powerful force to use and instigate new constructions in the mind and emotions to transform old patterns and establish new ones, therefore constantly creating new realities of existence.

+ The Theory of Creative Imagination has been used in all Metaphysical circles over ages of time. We certainly have been calling it to the attention of humanity through the last 100 years. Our modern communities began accepting it through:

  • Sports Advancement Theories

  • Biorhythm techniques for relaxing

  • Meditation (teaching the mind to expand from 3rd dimension)

  • Building from the energies of ethereal realms to focus and create a manifest in the realm of matter

This path connects the Creative Chaos of the Sphere of Wisdom to the containing power of the Sphere of Understanding, indeed into the birthing room for the manifestation to occur. Its color, Emerald Green, is the rich color of abundance, creativity, resourcefulness, love and nurturing. Do color your path in Illustration 2. Then, before we cover that sphere of Understanding, let us look at the other two pathways that exude from the Sphere of Wisdom: Worldly Development and Mastery.

PATH OF WORLDLY DEVELOPMENT

This path is the color of brilliant red and carries a power of assertion, pioneering the ways of the world, and developing the manifestations of a higher desire. The laws and order of the Universe are on the move with intention to build The Dream into a reality. The Dream of the Universe is to Individuate and allow all souls to explore and experience Allness. In the Allness are Worlds upon Worlds, Galaxies upon Galaxies, trillions of experiences, and more. We are only able to express the tip of the iceberg, at this point. As our consciousness continues to expand, we will, however, be expressing ever more awareness of this vast Universe and the Divine Mind creating it all. I am personally thrilled with the Quantum theorists who have been proving what mystics have been teaching.

This path is considered the window or Eye of the Divine, overseeing Its creation that is an ongoing, everchanging reality. This is a path of initiation that exudes, passion, fertility, a pioneering quality that gives rise to the leadership in all living creatures. It is called, "Creation's Dawn" as it exudes the power of God releasing Its voice in a modulated mantra of: "There was, I will Be, Let there Be, I Am that I Am." The sounds and modulation amplify the creative vibrations of manifestation. It is God calling forth His Dream into worldly development. As Source is sounding, It is calling forth the intent to bring order out of chaos. It is setting the tone and timbre of existence to establish, compose and organize the structure of all Living Substance.

You use this state of intelligence emanating from this path to establish order from the chaotic atmosphere of creative ideas. You set up your life boundaries so you may accomplish what you need. You do this by composing a plan and defining and formulating the structure of your dreams. You begin to use logic and deduce what is needed to accomplish your manifestation. If you create the dream to fulfill an educational program, you set out the plan to enter the school of choice, establish the course of study for the subjects needed, fulfill the monetary fees for entering the course work and establish the day and time of classes. You enter the field of study and undergo the task of completing the field of knowledge you are to glean over 2-4 years of study, or more. In fact, you use this corresponding formula to bring order for the fulfillment of any dream you have.

The Law of this path is the Law of Worldly Development. This law reiterates the choice of Source to manifest itself through the corridors of Matter. The Universal impulse creates the quiver of positive and negative poles, instigating the power of contracting and repelling vibrations that stimulate the current of action and materialization. In fact, notice that this path leads to a Central and Neutral Point on the matrix of the Tree of Life that is called Beauty, or the Higher Self of Humanity. (See Illustration 1.)

When you are working with this Law, you reveal an attribute to create and develop. You set plans into order and set a course of action. You attract and repel ideas until the one right idea is set to structure your plan into a materialized reality. You constantly keep a focus on your goal by being skilled in the area of your desire and maintain the right use of your Will Power and attitude of knowing you can create your own reality. You develop your manifest, step-by-step and use a constant forward motion to keep you stimulated and practicing your power as a leader and manifestor of dreams. Most certainly, the next path can help you as it calls forth the Mastery of personal consciousness.

PATH OF MASTERY

From Wisdom to Mercy, the Path of Mastery is formed. It releases a Reddish-Orange color releasing an active, creative innocence with a pure attitude of life mastery. In fact, a descent from the Holy Trinity is occurring with wisdom carried into the Higher Consciousness of Individuals. The power of Life Mastery is encoded in the soul-cell of all living creatures. The decoding of mastery comes through the agency of an Inner Voice and is sometimes felt as an Inner Teacher by us humans. Higher Wisdom and the awareness of the Purpose of All existence is released into this pathway.

This energy is often accessed through the feelings of Glorification and Honor of Source. The sense within you that knows everything is perfect, and is felt. This is a path that activates Inner Gnosis (the power to know).

This power is gained by:

- Intuition and Deduction (Reasoning)
- Testing and Discovering
- Meditating and Applying the Wisdom gleaned
- Listening to the Soul Voice and Responding
- Following the Laws of the Universe with awareness

This power is misused by:

- Use of only the Intuition Mind (leaving you in La La Land)
- Use of only the Reasoning Mind (believing that what you see in the physical realm is all there is)
- Meditating and then conveniently forgetting what was given
- Listening to the soul but not responding for fear that your outer world will not accept what your soul directs.
- Ignoring the Laws and misdirecting the energy

It is the virtue of this path to endure your existence through the power of Love. This endurance provides the ability to use the Law of this path, which is the Law of Life Mastery. Life Mastery occurs when you create a functioning harmony between the conscious mind and the subconscious mind. This opens the power to develop individual levels of proficiency and skillfulness used to navigate life. In so doing, the human form is able to Master its 3rd dimensional reality and learn more of its multi-dimensional existence.

Activating this Law with conscious focus:

✦ Know that you and every individual has something to master

✦ Master the following areas of your life

- Body
- Mind
- Emotions
- Interpersonal relationships
- Soul Purpose
- Spiritual Intent

Mastering your Body

✦ Directing its course rather than a separate body consciousness directing your habits

- Eating what sustains the body's health
- Practicing healthy fitness routines
- Cleansing and grooming
- Healthy sexual activities
- Understanding and eliminating addictive behaviors (which usually keeps us Earth bound whether the addiction is eating, sexuality, drugs, alcohol, spending, reading, computer use, cell phones, etc.)
- Raising the Vibration of your Body by releasing Collective Beliefs

Mastering your Mind

- ✦ Directing the patterns of thinking and educating
  - Keeping the mind alert and awake (most of the time we are sleeping while appearing awake)
  - Directing growth intentions
  - Directing the unconscious
  - Educating
  - Stimulating by remaining in the moment and curious about the Whole

Mastering your Emotions

- ✦ Emotions are a huge key to manifestation and need to be checked as they can create or break the power of manifestation. Therefore, it is important to overcome and master:
  - Over sensitivity
  - Under sensitivity
  - Stuck in the past or future with perceptions or hopes
  - The ability to heal the Past and remain in the Present to create your future
  - The ability to know that you are in charge of your feelings – NO ONE ELSE IS!

Mastering your Interpersonal Relationships

- ✦ Understanding the Purpose of Relating
  - Reflection of Self through others
  - Self Understanding
  - Ability to Share
  - Compassion
  - Reconciliation of Love seemingly lost by incarnation
  - Learning why you are in a relationship with a particular person (spouse, lover, friend, child, boss, peer, etc.)
  - That No One and Nothing Stands in your way (except yourself)
  - Movement beyond belief in Victimization

Mastering Soul Purpose

- ✦ Why are you here?
- ✦ Listening from within and living what you hear beyond personal judgement and fears
- ✦ Living with Soul Intent - Higher Will Power

Mastering Spiritual Intent

- ✦ Understanding the Universal Principles
- ✦ Living the Universal Principles
- ✦ Devotion to Higher Consciousness
  - • Living as though Higher Consciousness Matters
  - • Living as though Source Consciousness Matters
  - • Living Sacred Attitudes
  - • Living Source

The vice that exudes the challenges on this path is living with unworthiness and impoverishment. There is truly nothing on the Tree of Life that reveals to humanity that they must be poor in spirit, mind, emotion, or physical realities. In fact, the Tree of Life reports abundance on all levels and releases an understanding that poverty is a state of using the shadow side of the Laws of the Universe through allowing unconscious beliefs, brought about through doubt and fear, to dictate life events. If we want to know what the SIN of life is (Self Inflicted Negativity), it is that we do not accept our Mastery and the reality that we are Source personified in a human body.

When each of us take seriously the gift of Mastery, we create a change in our human world. We take on the clarity that we are creators, and we begin to release the fears and limitations that tell us we cannot be creators. We can affirm all day that we are Masters, however, if we are not clearing the inner consciousness, the affirmations seem to fall into an abyss and once again we experience distortions or abortions of our dreams.

In metaphysics, it is recognized that cellular memory can be cleared and then life changes are dynamic. All of our life experiences are contained in our cellular memory and take up at least 2/3rds of cellular consciousness used every day to manifest desires. The philosophy of meta-energy dictates that at least 2/3rds of our cellular memory must vibrate at the same thought, experience, emotion and desire to effect a change and create a new state of manifestation.

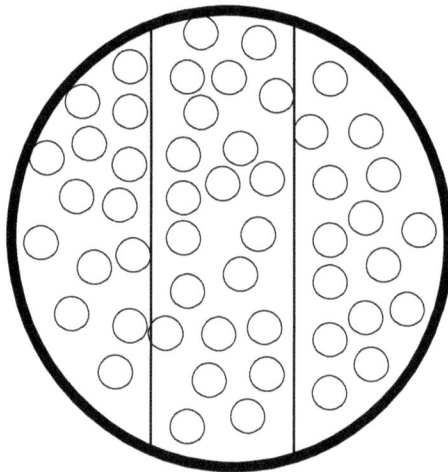

ILLUSTRATION 7. 1/3RD - 2/3RD THEORY MODEL

Most of us are living at more than 2/3rds vibration of challenging memories. It is important to shift the memory to align with our Soul Desire – to be Whole. In our desires, we may have 1/3rd of the cells vibrating to our new awareness, however, unless we have 2/3rds vibrating at the new thought, we only see partial results of our positive dream. The repetition of the old patterns keep showing up because 2/3rds of our memory cells are connected to the old thoughts and old vibrations of toxic memory.

I have found that personal awareness and Chakra therapy helps clear the old vibrational memory, opens you to direct, positive vibrations and frees your Will Power to fill the cells with affirmative intent. The positive cellular memory will take over and the empowered response to Life Mastery can be the results.

3rd Sphere - Understanding

The final sphere of the Supernal Triad is a deep indigo color at the level of its creative world, and represents the Womb of the Universe. It is the Divine Feminine Principle and mostly known as Goddess. Though, in our Christian era we call this Essense, Mother Mary or the Virgin Mother. She is known through other philosophies as Sophia, Quan Yin, Anu and many other names.

This sphere of consciousness is the first order of Containing the Uncontainable. It absorbs the creative expression of Chaos and defines its cellular expression into the extension of what it is to become: A galaxy, angel, human, animal, plant, mineral, etc. . . Perhaps it is to be the light or the dark, matter or gases. It is from this level of consciousness that faith is encoded, words are defined and time and space are formulated. It is from this sphere of consciousness a "Beginning" occurs; the beginning of defining the Undefinable Universe (a tremendous paradox to ponder). In the Tree of Life philosophy, it is noted that at this stage of Creation, the Individuation, named Soul, is made known. The Children of the Father/Mother Source is set for birthing into the realm of matter. The pure image is to be the perfect model of God/Goddess.

This sphere of consciousness provides the receptive power of Creation and is pure as well as purifying. Its virtue is Faith which is a power encoded in every living creator. To have this encoded in the very essence of your individual self provides an awareness that you are never left without faith. You may be left without trust, but never without faith. This is why you keep on going, even when life's challenges seem unsurmountable.

The sphere of Understanding represents what Stands Under Source and is Its Foundation and Structure. It is the initiating point of the Pillar of Form which ignites the power of insight and foresight as well as the ability to make Holy, to complete an intention.

It also initiates the Power of Separation. Motion away from Source or Outward Motion ignites the spiral and the experience of moving away from One in order to experience the Many. This power provides patterns set to contain form of a particular design.

As the spiral effect continues, the creation of Mental Powers distinguishes objects of thought and one thought from another. This establishes boundaries and limits turning inner consciousness outward to manifestation which:

◆ Forms

◆ Defines

◆ Limits

◆ Specializes

◆ Labels

As Substance (Mass + Space = Matter) is formed, it allows us (soul) to be present and recognizable as an individual. It supports the entire universe and provides form, color, time, life and death to be experienced.

This Sphere of Understanding is the Foundation of Primordial Wisdom and is the Ruler of Life; the Mother of All. It is known as Virgin Mother - Sterile Mother (Before Form). The voidless void. It is a passive essence in its sterile form. It is also the Fertile Mother revealing Light in Darkness, Masculine and Feminine joining (Sphere 2 and 3) and producing Form. It is Receptive Fertility—the Womb of the Universe.

At the Point of Understanding All Forms Originate:

✦ Divine Soul

✦ Creation of Faith Occurs

✦ The word "Amen" is an acknowledgment and a stirring of Faith to rise from your encoded reality.

✦ Time and Matter exudes from this sphere of consciousness and allows for involution and evolution to occur; the experience of life and death and ultimately the final resting place and return to Oneness.

✦ Language that will be used in words and phrases to identify existence

Archangel Tzaphkiel, is the form of consciousness that holds the Matrix of Understanding in its perfect order. She is seen as the Archangel of the Archetypal Temple (All Archetypes) and represents the:

✦ Contemplation of Source

✦ Overseer of Life and Death – Evolutionary Cycle

✦ Overseer of Good and Evil (Duality)

✦ Teacher of Life

This angelic being is the Teacher of Teachers and is constantly helping each person define the cycles of life and the polarities of experience that is occurring. Tzaphkiel encourages each person to understand the powers of Dedication, Discipline, Determination and Devotion, the four elements that assist in bringing non-matter to matter; or the creative desire into a manifest form.

It is from this Sphere of Consciousness that Source releases Itself into individuation. It releases Its Likeness, which is Everything. It provides a microscopic look at every cell of Its existence: planets and stars, Sun and Moon, humans and non-humans, and so forth. Out of the darkness comes the Light of Many Colors and the schematic of every living soul. (Whether that be man or woman, animal or plant, desk or computer, car or highway, house or garden, etc. Soul is everything.)

It is within this state of Consciousness that you may find the agency of nurturing, the power of the pure archetype of your dreams and desires, and the structural design of causal vibrations waiting for you to draw from and create the foundation of all things you wish to achieve. The Ray of Understanding passes from this agency of Universal Consciousness and provides you with the means of knowing you Stand Under Source and are the Foundation of Source. To know this, you will want to use the Virtue of this sphere, which is Silence. Sacred Silence. The ability to quiet your emotions, mind, body and ego so you may hear the voice within and be directed by the Voice of Source. And the experience of this Silence calls you to say, "Amen," which means, "It Is So"!

Three light rays illuminate paths from this Sphere. The path of Creative Imagination, already spoken of, is a fluidic moving path, releasing energy between Wisdom and Understanding and back again. The Seeds of Life from Wisdom enter the womb of the Universe through the doorway of Soul Emanations and form a distinction in the realm of Understanding. The individuated quality of Source, known as Soul, travels back and forth from creative chaos to containment and back and forth extracting more wisdom to use the gift of the unique and loving power of Divine Mind.

Descending from Understanding is the path of Discernment and the Path of Containment. These pathways enter the realm of the Triad of the Avatar, the Higher Self of Humanity. They assist in providing energy from Above and defining energy to be used by you to help you develop and guide your life and your variety of purposes to fulfill. The first path to exit this sphere is called Discernment and a much needed power to assist you to unfold the right steps and points of life that will help you define the final manifest you desire. The path of Containment calls you to set the boundaries necessary to hold the matrix of your desires in an order of usefulness and expression.

PATH OF DISCERNMENT

From this path Source initiated Free Will and Choice, which is defined and encoded in the cellular system of each individual creation (Soul) of Source Consciousness. This is an "automatic" process sealed within every being. As each soul births into the Rite of Individuation, the power to choose its direction and evolutionary scheme is set upon them.

A devotional intelligence is released as well, providing a power to remember the One True Self and the Highest Order of Creation. It stimulates the devotion to persevere. It is a vibration that calls for the Devout State of Consciousness within the Soul of all living creatures.

- ◆ Devout
  - • One Devoted to a Higher Power

- One who has persevered to bring their Thoughts, Emotions and Actions into harmony with Universal Consciousness. (Requires keen discernment)

- Through devotion, one has an ability to understand the concept of duality (division into two opposed or contrasted aspects, such as good and evil or mind and matter) and/or polarity (the state of having poles or opposites, such as positive ions and negative ions), as it is associated with the Divine, as well as with the individual self.

+ Hidden mystery is revealed to the Devout as they follow this path

  - Nothing is without understanding when one is devoted to exploring, discerning and defining what IS.

+ Spiritual Alchemy

  - Discernment provides an awareness that Enlightens. Enlightenment is the ingredient that stirs the alchemy of oneness and wholeness (nothing more, nothing less)

How you Use this Path

+ Through Right Discernment:

  - Express an ability to assess your life with clarity and without negative judgment based on fears

  - Learn through experiences

  - Evaluate situations, circumstances and events in your life and how they are helping you grow through challenges or rewards without making

them right or wrong; simply understanding they
are a part of your soul quest

- Evaluate how you are using the wisdom you are
gaining in any situation (with another; with a
concept, with an action, with a project, etc.)

- Gain an ability to separate the wheat from the
chaff (value from non-value). For instance:

    - Worry is not of value

    - Immediate awareness is valuable

    - Being nosey is not of value

    - Discerning your own position in life is valuable

The Law of Union is activated on this path. This law provides the wisdom that everything (matter or non-matter) is
made of the one atom – the Atom of Source. Therefore, everything is in Union by nature. We are all One Cell expressing
individual qualities of The Cell – Source. We are God/Goddess
in Matter and Self in the Non-Matter of God/Goddess.   We
are the Living Source and, individually, we affect each other.
We affect Source and Source affects us. We are never separate
from Source, we are in constant and ever-lasting Union.

This law is carried onto this pathway as the Souls are
spewed from the Great Mother and delivered into their
kingdom.

- ✦ It causes you to remember Oneness when Duality/
Polarity occurs (Birth into Human consciousness).

- ✦ It provides the power to unify with others, situations
and events.

- ✦ It provides the power to assess the journey a soul

takes as it passes over the Abyss and appears to lose memory of Oneness.

✦ The Power of the Creator provides the Soul with the ability to realize that the illusion of separateness is only the effect produced by the One Great Self "concentrating its limitless energy at any particular point in time and space."

✦ As a soul transcends its limits of human qualities, it forms a union with Its Divine qualities. This union enlivens and enlightens the individuation and an assessment occurs that allows the Soul to form a Union with the Holy Trinity. This union empowers you.

The power of Discernment and Devotion help you utilize, most effectively, the next path that is a ray of light emanating from the 3rd sphere and providing yet another vibration for your soul's journey to use. As you have likely surmised, the power of living individual qualities has opened up and the dream and desire that you really, really, really want to manifest is aided by the use of the wisdom of each sphere and each path now being explored. Take some time to think about how the quality of evolving consciousness can and is already helping you formulate an outcome of what you want. Then, proceed with the next path and prepare to enter the next Triad.

PATH OF CONTAINMENT

You learned in the 3rd sphere that the energy of Creative Chaos that exudes from the 2nd sphere has to be contained in order to be identified, individualized and put to use in the form of matter. This path continues to explore this conscious state and helps the individual quality of soul-experiences to evolve.

This path formulates the power of consciousness that defines and contains the archetypal design of the vehicle that will be used to manifest the Holy Spirit. This field of energy contains Spirit's intention to form and unite each soul with a personal expression (your personality), as well as maintain the enclosure of the Essence of Source within the Holy Temple (your body of existence in any incarnation).

Encoded in this path of consciousness is the Original Covenant of Source. The Covenant is the plan and ultimate agreement to maintain Oneness through the agency of Individuation. As the Soul leaves the Womb of the Divine, it is encased in this agreement and ensconced in the Oneness.

The Law of Containment is activated on this path. It provides the energy that forms synthesis of matter and non-matter, passive and active energy, and the fusion of boundaries in a boundaryless Universe. The quality of boundary provides the ways and means to use the wisdom and vibrancy of Source.

You are constantly using this law and it is revealed by containment and use of your inner power. You reveal this containment by setting the parameters of experiences and expressing through parameters you set.

The parameters you set bring about self-awareness and therefore self-expression. It is very important that you know yourself and share yourself with others by setting of boundaries, so you may live victoriously on your Life Path.

This path releases the power of speech and the Logos of the Universe translated through you. It is important that you:

- ✦ Know that your words hold power
- ✦ Speech Defines - Be sure to say what you mean
- ✦ Words used ritually, prayerfully, and in mantra form and calls you to initiate a:
    - Union with the Divine - Calling forth Higher Fusion of Energy with personal consciousness
    - Supplication of Desire - Activating Creative Imagination
    - Sealing the Energy - Always through Gratitude
    - Manifesting - drawing down the perfect design of Source

When you utilize this pathway to manifest what you really want, you must form your boundaries, define your desire, then speak out what you want. In fact, take some time to define and then speak out loud, forming energy with universal consciousness that brings order and the container for the right outcome to occur.

Use the virtue of this pathway, which is Surrender, to support your outcome. Choose to surrender (become receptive) to the higher vision of your Soul journey, and verbalize your gratitude for all expressions to be manifest from the mind and heart of Source. Be careful not to get involved in the vice of the shadow of this path which is disappointment, struggle and false beliefs being held as true. These challenges always cause you to distort or abort your desired outcome.

Keep your parameters of expression clearly in your awareness. Know what you can do and what you cannot do each day, so you do not over-extend yourself and fall out of clarity and direct alignment with the purpose of your desire. Speak only of the outcome you want and leave all other words in the ethers of non-expression.

Take a moment to review the three spheres and the eight pathways that emanate from the Supernal Triad, imposing an energy of manifestation, and initiating the qualities of individual reflections of Source. Review again how this Living Tree is a guiding force, but also the energy of yourself living in matter. It is from this Supernal state of Consciousness that All things flow. Source descends into individuated states and moves Its Countenance into the realm of the Avatar Triad.

APPLE ORCHARD OF SOURCE

Just imagine, for a moment, the beauty of the Garden of Eden. Fall is in the air. Crisp and delightful breezes flow through the trees. The Apple Orchards are ready to be harvested. Great smells from the kitchen of the Creator waft with the aroma of apples and cinnamon. Apples, a significant symbol of Spirit, keep our attention alert to the story of the Garden of Eden. Of course, we know of Eve and the Apple Tree and the perceived Fall from this blissful state. Ah, but do we know the true significance of this? Here is a thought-provoking story.

Adam and Eve are living in paradise. Life is blissful. Their parents, God and Goddess, watch them wander through the gardens, but see boredom in their children's expression. Nothing is happening. No use of the creative minds they were given can be detected. There is an appearance of contentment, but their eyes are glazed and they move about the garden like drones. The Great Mother/Father observed that Adam and Eve weren't creating anything. Everything was there for them. They needed nothing.

God and Goddess decided to change that reality and slipped an encouragement through the gate of intuition (feminine) and called for Eve to check out the Tree of Knowledge of Good and Evil (polarities) and learn how a transformation could occur (snake) to release passion and creative urges. Eve, delightfully inspired, opened to the power of creative possibilities immediately. After being smitten by the enlightenment of transformation, Eve wanted to share it with Adam (Masculine - Logic). Though first denying the temptation (denying intuition), Adam did eat of this fruit.

At that very point, God and Goddess rejoiced. "Ah, our children have opened the door of Free Will and Choice." The gift of polarities (reward and challenge) initiated the power to Fall (evolve) into the world of matter and explore the creative powers of Source through a myriad of experiences.

The Apple became a known fruit in the realm of matter and provided a secret within it. For when cut in half horizontally, a Five-Pointed Star appears in the inner circle of the fruit. This was and is to always remain as the symbolic memory that Adam and Eve (and all individuals) are sacred human beings – the Divine Children held in the Sacred Womb (circle) of the Goddess. This is and was to always help the creations of Source remember that they are in the Garden of Eden. They are simply now exploring every part of it and using each part to create and manifest just as God/Goddess does.

Taking a big breath, God and Goddess released their children, again and again, into the never ending galaxies and planetary forms of Itself. The State of Earth consciousness, they surmise, best suits the power of creativity, the wisdom of discovery, and the gift of evolving to gain back memory that all people are the offspring of Source. Source simply wants the creative experience to be known in the individual state, which is the Bliss of the Great Creator.

Enjoy your apples, the fruit of Source, as you continue to explore the Living Tree.

Part II

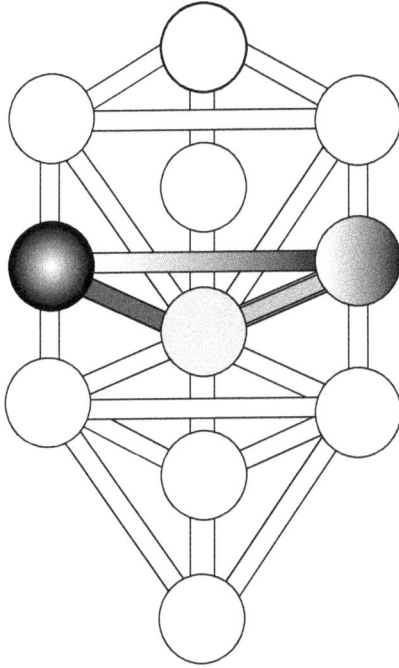

The Higher Self Triad

Higher Self/Avatar Triad and Pathways

VEIL: DESTINY AND EVOLUTION

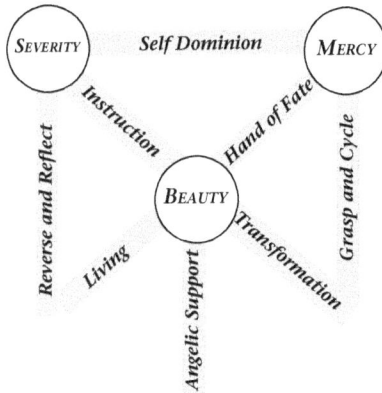

The descent now carries the Soul across a threshold, a *Veil of Destiny,* and into an enchanting range of consciousness. The philosophy of the Tree of Life asserts that the Divine Parents, birthing all individuated states of life, release each soul into their individual and independent stages of growth and an evolution of experiences. As good parents, they send their children off to their destiny well equipped, as we will uncover in this Triad of Wisdom.

As the story unfolds, the Supernal Consciousness is recognized as the Royal Monarch and called the 'Supreme Being.' We know that children of a monarch inherit the position as Sovereign, and take the crown, wealth and attributes of the head of the throne.

In the model of the Tree of Life, everything flows downward from the top of the tree (crown) and extends into every sphere and pathway. That means the Un-namable Supreme Being of All Life presents all of Its Glory into all other states of being. The Divine Father/Mother Explodes into the Activity of:

+ Many Souls – All Living Creatures
+ Action of Divine Conscious Intelligence flowing to Individual States of Being
+ Universal Intent put into Unconscious Reality (meaning automatic living)
+ All Universal Laws automatically flow through every soul and all existence

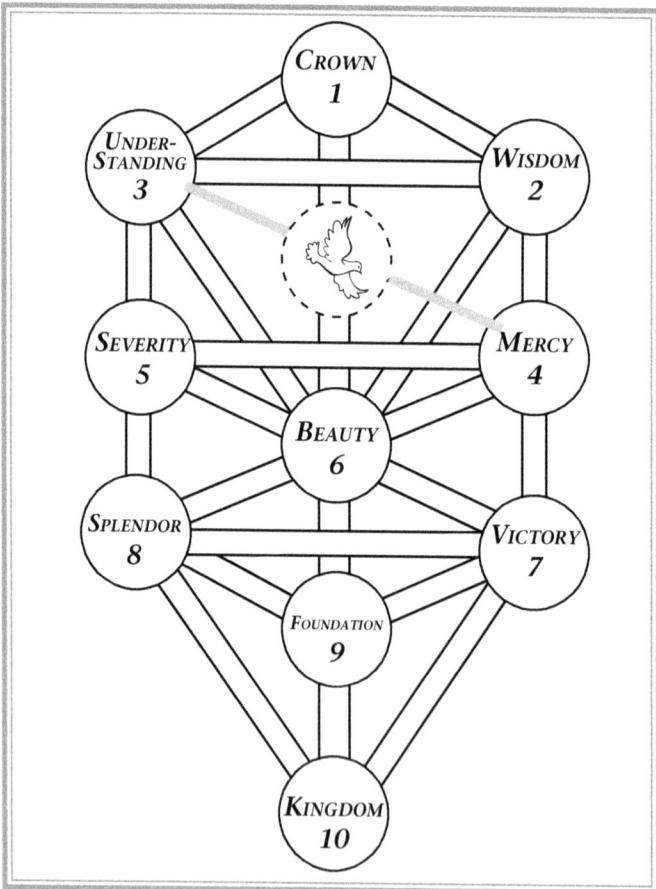

ILLUSTRATION 8: DESCENT OF THE HOLY SPIRIT

Illustration 8 of the Tree of Life shows the Veil of Destiny of Evolution as it is rent. The presentation of the Supreme Being flows into the individuated qualities of all living creatures as a Dove shown as the Holy Spirit descending. This flow moves into the Higher-Self Triad and releases *All That Is* to the children to inherit.

The Christian story takes this into the Child, Jesus of Nazareth, who inherits the qualities of God and distributes them to the Earth. Other Avatars are given the same story. Buddha most certainly is seen as an Avatar (a deity released into bodily form). He inherited all wisdom and distributed these gifts of enlightenment to the world.

The philosophy of the Tree of Life carries a more profound secret that implies we are all avatars and simply have entered a vehicle called a body, a 'Holy Living Temple.' As a Light of the Supreme Being, we are encased in this Holy Living Temple so we may move through, experience and utilize individual qualities of the Supreme Parents (the Feminine Principle and Masculine Principle of Source). As inheritors of all qualities of Source, we like all Avatars, can express Divine wisdom, health, wealth and all that may be needed in the realm of matter.

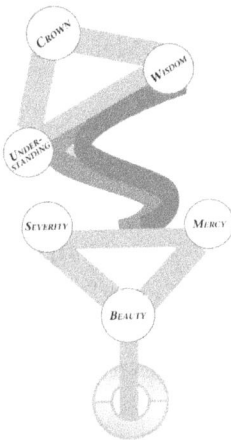

The first order of the journey of Descent into Destiny causes us to focus on the three spheres of consciousness in the Higher-Self Triad with the focal point being Beauty. The triangular shape of this triad has its focal point flowing downward, which is a reversal of the Supernal Triad. This mystery is revealed as the Universal Consciousness reversing Itself from non-matter or sole expression to matter forming in multiple expressions. The Grail Cup is created and the fluidic Light of Source, individualized, is contained and expressing as a Soul-child.

These vibrant masses of whirling light in the second triad are identified as:

✦ Mercy: The Great Beneficent

Deemed: The Presentation of All that is Needed

✦ Severity: The Great Protector

Deemed: The Purification and Solidification of the archetypal expressions of Source

✦ Beauty: The Higher Self

Deemed: Throne of the Child Avatar

Rays of light emanate from the spheres of consciousness, and as pathways, emit the vibration of power to be used by the individuated forms of Source. The energy of Source (the Crown in the Supernal Triad) takes another path into the Triad of the Higher-Self as It flows through the path of Love, swirls uncontrollably in the Sphere of Wisdom, spins into the path of Mastery and spills into the Sphere of Mercy, activating the Avatar consciousness.

From Mercy, we find the pathway that provides the power to live in Self-Dominion. We also experience the extended Hand of Fate (Source) and grasp it.

From the Sphere of Severity (which receives energy from Source through the realm of Understanding and the path of Containment), the awareness of Self-Dominion takes on the flow of allowing instruction of Source to be extended to the consciousness of the Higher-Self and the wisdom to reverse the power of Source into the realm of matter. From the central focus of Beauty, energy flows and descends, teaching the power of transformation, the wisdom of living in all dimensions, and the awareness that each soul travels the realms with angelic support. Each path provides an automatic use of a universal law that will be discussed as we journey through the wisdom of this Triad of the Higher-Self.

As you continue to focus on what you *really, really, really* want, the spheres remind you that all you desire is seeded within your Higher-Self. As you will see through the three spheres of the Higher-Self Triad and the Pathways, you are required to accept the gifts of Source, transform them to the realm of matter through honoring your Higher-Self and maintaining dominion over your mind, emotions and actions. Be assured that your focus will bring everything you are focused on into fruition. Keep your intent to manifest clear of clutter such as fear, doubt and lack of clarity.

SPHERE 4 - MERCY

This mass of light swirls from the Creative World and shimmers in the color of royal blue. Action on the Pillar of Force emanates the vibration of Love from the Holy Father to His Child. Contained within this Vibration is everything that will ever be needed on the journey of evolution (from non-matter to matter and back to non-matter). Subsistence, which remains in force and effect eternally, is provided. Security and the power to grow and vibrate in every cell of memory, encoded in the unit called the Soul – your Soul.

This Sphere of Mercy is also the middle point on the Pillar of Force, creating a station of importance and a place of balance. It integrates the sphere below it with the sphere above it. Mercy is a sphere of building and constructing the matrix of all living matter.

God, the Benevolent, is lovingly activating all of Its substance into the individual quality of life through this whirling sphere. In fact, when I teach classes on the Tree of Life, I often call this sphere the "Santa Claus" sphere of influence. Joy, abundance, and all that is good are presented for the soul to use. The power of unconditional love, the creative abilities to source your life with the health and wealth that you will need is found in the matrix of this sphere. In fact, anything and everything that you could possibly desire, and more, is provided through this station of consciousness. And the beauty is, it is encoded within you.

Within your own nature is the attitude of lovingly supporting others. You carry the intent to do no harm, produce all that is good, bring generosity into activities of life and promote the welfare of love and happiness. You also feel the benevolence of Source when you remember the loving support that moves through you or is seen by you through the graces of others (emissaries of Source). All that you need, and will ever need, is truly in a treasure chest within you. Your faith releases it, your focus details it, and your willingness to contain it in matter provides the use of anything and everything you desire.

Held within this station of consciousness is the binding force of Unconditional Love. It releases the higher motivational factor within all. It stirs satisfaction and harmony. It releases a knowing within the Soul that these qualities must be experienced by the individual in order to present it to all others.

Pure and unadulterated creative power is released from Mercy. This pristine energy is used to create the foundation

for the perfect idea to be used by the individual consciousness. To assist in this use, a cohesive state of consciousness is
embedded in the soul. This cohesiveness

+ Receives the Holy Spirit

+ Administers the Principles of Understanding

+ Contains the Aura of Source (Rings: Cosmos, Chaos
  and Pass Not)

+ Brings pieces and parts of the Whole together

The Virtue of this sphere is Obedience. We understand
obedience to mean to follow an authority – Divine Authority. However, it also means to carry out the Order of the Universe by living according to the Principle of the Law(s) – more
succinctly, the Law of Love, and of course, all other Laws aris-
ing from the Law of Love.

The vices of this sphere are Waste, Bigotry and/or Tyranny. It is important to realize that we are given everything.
It is contained within us and we must simply bring it forward by our intent, integrity, and above all, love. We waste
the energy of Grace when we deny the force of love and the
beauty of creative powers releasing all that we need. We are
bigots when we display prejudice to anything. However, we
must know that when we display a lack of belief in the gift of
Source, we display a preconceived opinion that is not based
on truth and therefore we display prejudice against the Fa-
ther/Mother of All. Tyranny is expressed by us through cruel
or arbitrary attitudes of controlling others and not allowing
the Source power to flow through every circumstance. We
lock ourselves into belief systems that our persona dictates
believing our human laws and our judgments are the only
correct ones. We forget the power of the Universal Laws allowing Higher Consciousness to move within our every in-

tent. We let the Universal Laws envelop us by our dictates and often find the challenge or vice of the Law manifesting. The Laws flow unconditionally, yet positively or negatively, according to our focus, attitudes and actions. They are automatic and all Laws are enveloped in Cause and Effect.

Cause and Effect:

+ Love and you are loved

+ Withhold Love and Love is withheld from you

+ Contemplate Source and you are Source

+ Contemplate Separation and you are Separate

+ Let Light emanate from you and you are Light

+ Live in Darkness and Darkness Lives in you

To help find the perfect balance and the wisdom of this sphere, Archangel Tzadkiel reveals the Matrix of the Benevolence of God. From Tzadkiel, we receive the wisdom of Divine Justice. Archangel Tzadkiel provides everything needed for our growth and maintenance. He contains the force of this Sphere of Consciousness, expands limits and expands the giving of all that is needed. As we gain personal awareness and responsible natures for manifesting our desires, more is given. Tzadkiel follows the edict of Source to not give more than we can handle.

Archangel Tzadkiel helps us perfect as we grow by providing inspiration and direction for right action. Through a benevolent inner voice, he prompts the search for truth and helps everyone grow to a higher level of awareness. He helps us understand the Power of Discernment that aids in learning how to keep everything balanced versus gorging on too much of anything. Using the gift of teaching through loving acts, intuition and intellect are brought to symmetry.

Archangel Tzadkiel can point the way, inspire and direct energy through inner prompting; but we must heed the directive of our own accord and proceed on the path at our own pace. Archangel Tzadkiel:

+ Cannot create the pace for us or we will remain unwise children on the path of return

+ Can inspire – but we must use the inspiration

+ Teaches us that we cannot experience new things while holding onto old realities

+ Teaches that we cannot hold an old and new pattern at the same time and expect a new experience to come of it

+ Reveals that a painful process exists if we try to hold onto old concepts while attempting to express a new one (the old holds us back)

The loving power of the Sphere of Mercy, repeatedly calls us inward to renew our Spirit with Source Consciousness. This releases us back into balance and prepares us to use the Gifts of Source. Then, our personal consciousness vibrates through the pathways and discovers, uncovers and uses the powers within. Thus, the path of Self-Dominion, between Mercy and Severity, blesses and presents the ability to use the inner power.

PATH OF SELF-DOMINION

The brighter color of yellow welcomes us along this Path. From Mercy, we carry the vibration of all that we need, desire and want to manifest. Encoded within every cell of our Soul is the power to know exactly how to use these gifts. The Spiritual Fire within is ready to ignite our intentions and spur our energy to go and grow, shine and reveal the Sacred Being that we are.

Intelligence is embedded within each soul, called, "The Secret Works." It reveals that Creation is neither good nor bad, it simply IS. This 'Is-ness' exists in all life and therefore all life is spiritual. All activities are transmutations and conversions of Source. This allows us to seek without fear, judgment and concern. More secrets are revealed to the Seeker when she is ready to become aware and ready to express her Highest Quality.

- ✦ Secrets can be uncovered by the student of life through the agency of education that includes:
  - Spiritual Disciplines
  - Angelology
  - Astrology
  - Colorology
  - Numerology
  - All levels of Symbology
  - Educational systems (Universities of: Theology, Science, Psychology, etc.)

- ✦ Secrets are revealed via:
  - Averting Ignorance (study)
  - Meditation (go beyond human levels of consciousness)

- Contemplation (willingness to do inner awareness work by thinking about the meaning of things)
- Maintaining a sacred discipline

This path is embedded with the Law of Self-Dominion. Use of this law opens the doorway to the revelation of secrets. This law is inscribed within each soul releasing the ability to be self-governing, live in harmony with the Supreme Power and Authority that exists within Itself and its environment.

✦ To gain the awareness of this Supreme Authority one must:

- Use fortitude to discover Self
- Understand one's natural self and live it rather than a façade
- Understand the sub-conditions of consciousness

  - Personal memory

  - Personal fears and sabotaging attitudes

  - Personal strengths not yet discovered

  - Power of Source Living Within

- Understand the super-conditions of consciousness

  - Higher Self

  - Divine Consciousness

  - Perfect wisdom

- Modify personal self to align with Higher-Self
- Live in the power of purity – Freedom from Mixture

The mixture of the three levels of consciousness brings the Cognitive, Subconscious and Super-Consciousness into One Active Conscious State. It provides the union of personal consciousness, collective conscious and Supernal Consciousness. When these combinations act as one, we are in the state of 'At-One-ment.' (Atonement – The reconciliation of God/Goddess and Humankind).

This pathway calls for a balance between the Pillars of Force and Form and the Spheres of Mercy and Severity. Before we capture the meaning of the Sphere of Severity, we will review the other rays of light emanating from Mercy.

PATH OF THE HAND OF FATE

This pathway releases the color of Yellow-Green. It is the vibration emitting the outstretched hand of Source, providing everything that is needed to the sovereign child. The power of Fate is the reality that all you need is already encoded and ready to be experienced. Free Will and Choice allow you to reach for the hand and receive the gifts that the Inner Will, Source-Soul impulses that create urges of life to be experienced. If it is joy one moment, creativity the next, challenges within it all, and so forth, the Hand of Fate provides each, unconditionally and with ultimate support of love.

This pathway helps you understand the encoded reality of Fate and how you are using it. It connects Mercy with Beauty (the throne of the Crowned Child). It reveals the wisdom the Light of Guidance offers to connect you with the Primordial Point of Source.

This path represents the self-sustained original beginnings of Manifestation and is the reward of thought, emotions and actions maintaining congruity and forming the manifested realities of dreams and desires. It carries the Intelligence of Will – the Will of Creator.

◆ It prepares all created beings, individually, for the demonstration of the existence of the Primordial Glory

• Oneness with the Primal Self

◆ This path forms the patterns of All things that are, will be and are yet to develop.

When aligned and identified with this Primal Will, one can identify with the Avatar consciousness:

• Christ/Moses/Buddha/Kuan Yin/Mary

All Masters sought not to live from their personal will, but from the Primal Will of the One sending him into his experiences. Allowing your personal will to release the Primal Will strengthens and empowers you. When you align with Primal Will, you form a great concentration and can easily express as a channel for Divine Right Action in your life.

To activate this power within you, be responsive. Know you have the ability to turn and move beyond the beliefs and limitations that your personal world offers. Center your thoughts, emotions and actions on the wisdom of Wholeness.

The act of living with the Fate of Higher Purpose requires the intelligence (awareness) of your personal will and an ability to change it immediately when you discover it is not honoring positive function. If your personal will is walking a path of lack in any area (lack of integrity, lack of awareness, lack of love or being loved, lack of affluence, not allowing the universal energy to flow in all areas of your life, and so forth), you must be willing to change your direction of thought, feeling and action. It requires the fortitude of your will to live with higher intention. It requires you to use your ability to maintain a relationship with the Divine at such a level that you operate at that level with all people and events in your life, including your own Soul when at work, play, interpersonal relationships, social gatherings, at home in quiet, etc.

To help you meet these requirements, the Law of Wholeness is implanted in this path of consciousness. This Law reveals the constant truth that every soul is contained in the existence of All that Is and All that Is is contained in every soul. Every person, animal, plant, mineral and galactic essence is complete in and of itself and therefore, Whole. Of course, this provides us with the wisdom that:

- ✦ Existence of holism is within us and within our manifest world

- ✦ There is nothing we cannot manifest, for it already is

- ✦ The Universe, in Its holism, moves in and out, spirals and evolves and nothing is ever lost or gained as It is simply exploring Itself

- ✦ We are that exploration

- ✦ The exploration offers constant manifestation of ideas and desires

- ✦ We can learn of this holism and live it by practicing awareness of our S.E.M.P.E.S.

THE MEANING OF S.E.M.P.E.S.
(Spiritual, Emotional, Mental, Physical, Ego, Soul)

SPIRITUAL – This is your Vital Life Force Energy. It is indestructible. It is cause and effect occurring simultaneously within you. It maintains the atomic/subatomic, DNA/RNA of your soul. It is the essence that originated your soul and evolves through your personality. It is your Divine Aspect. You relate to it by expressing reverence, respect, love and honor for the Great Source of All Life. You recognize it in the beauty of all things.

EMOTIONAL – This is the essence of You that feels. It stimulates manifestation of the Vital Life Force. The emotional quality of You is active and plays an important part in forming the manifested world around you. It is the steering mechanism of your mental aspects in order to form the structure of your body from your subatomic cells right on to your tissue, organs, bones and skin. It is the protective housing of your Soul and the essence that helps you experience your soul-urging. It is the creative aspect of You. It provides the pattern of your moods, currents of your biorhythm, and your inner drive and desires for your evolution. It cannot be touched, nor can it be seen, but it can be deeply experienced through your feeling nature. You encounter it at surface levels and deeper inner levels. You know it through joy and sorrow, highs and lows, anger and love, elation and depression and every single mood you experience.

MENTAL – This is the essence of your intelligence. It is your conscious and unconscious thoughts. It is the aspect of You that directs the course of your emotions, formulates your imagination and inner experiences, and helps produce a manifest through the employment of creative imagination. You know it as your thinking, reasoning and the logical applications of your mind. It is the aspect of your thinking that brings about both positive and negative responses, for it is your trial, judge and jury of all activities you experience. Through your mental aspect you discern your joys and sorrows, your ability to create, intuit, learn, intellectualize and evaluate situations, circumstances or events. Using the function of your mind with your intuitive qualities, you can also learn how to empower telepathic communication.

PHYSICAL – This is the essence of your body and your physical environment. Through this aspect you use your senses of smell, taste, touch, sight and hearing. All uses of your body belong in the realm of the physical. Action through walking, running, swimming, biking, dancing, sexual activities and so forth, occur only through the physical realm. (Though at times you dream of these activities, the dreams are memories of your physical experiences). All physical experiences are a part of this aspect, including living in your home, working in your career, being with others, relating to the earth and the environment as a whole (sky, clouds, plants, animals, stones, etc.), experiencing weather, seasons, and so forth. Certainly it is evident that the physical aspect of you includes your organs, skin, bones, tissues and the wondrous flow of life-blood that carries your Vital Life Force energy throughout your physical system.

EGO – Although this aspect may be seen akin to the mental qualities of You, it is a facet replete in its own power. The ego is the outer expression of the inner You, and when evolved, it is the outer expression of your Higher-Self. It is the part of You that provides the energy to survive the human experience. It is the element of each of us that seeks to know more by learning about itself. Through self-learning, evolution occurs and achieving expressions of your Higher Beingness can be the result. Your ego can act as separatist, essence of fear, narcissistic and self-absorbed. It can also be bold, daring, forward moving, and express the dynamics of the Goddess-Being that you are.

SOUL – This aspect of You is the expression of the Divine Self as an individuated quality. It is the Spark of Life that has evolved through the eons of one life experience after another. Its function is to remember its entirety, remain on purpose, recall the vibrational frequencies it has experienced from one life to another and respond to its coding to return to the Goddess. You experience it through your inner sense of knowing, the urging to do and be, and the deep sense of recognizing a Great Power within that knows it is the expression of the Goddess.

As you integrate the S.E.M.P.E.S qualities, you initiate the power of wholeness and open up to the fate imprinted in your soul to accomplish its journey. You release the power to heal, balance, perform feats of genius and offer the gift of service to all others.

PATH OF GRASP AND CYCLE

As you connect with the Hand of Fate, you grasp it and begin the cycle and phases of soul-evolution with the purpose of experiencing the Higher Will. This path emits a violet ray of light. It represents the grasping hand as opposed to the open hand in the previous path. It is the continual reminder that when a hand is outstretched, it is important that we grasp it in order to receive the gifts being provided.

On this path, we integrate with the intelligence of the quest, the virtue of spiritual centering, empowerment of the

Higher Will, practicing and living Mastery and abiding in patience. In the polarity, we experience the vice of a spinning consciousness, living as others desire, abiding falsehood, expressing blatant judgment and the exploration of mood swings and impatience.

This branch on the tree prepares the consciousness to descend into the Soul Triad. In the preparatory state, Source Consciousness encases the Will-to-Quest into the individual soul. The quest, in the state of pseudo-separation, empowers the desire to seek Wisdom and the Knowledge, ultimately, of Source.

The "Seeker" is your soul as well as your personality.

+ Your Soul is seeking to know the Divine in all aspects as it involutes into the place of matter and evolves to the place of Spirit.

+ The Seeker aspect of your personality attempts to find "something" important to make its mark upon the world. Several phases of seeking occurs

  • Seeking Intelligence

  • Seeking the expression of Talents

  • Seeking the expression of Health

  • Seeking the expression of Importance/Viability

  • Seeking the expression of Wealth

  • Seeking Success

  • Seeking what it means to be Human (Question of the Sphinx)

The Sphinx at Thebes is the archetype of Supreme Enigma. It is carved with the head of a human, body of a bull/

ox, claws and tail of a lion and wings of a bird. It represents the uniting of the four elements (Fire, Water, Air, Earth), four directions (South, West, East and North), and four Cardinal Points in Astrology (Aries, Cancer, Libra, Capricorn).

✦ The Seeker ultimately is:
  • Seeking Peace and Love
  • Seeking Harmony with Others
  • Seeking Understanding of Life
  • Seeking Spiritual Awareness
  • Seeking Understanding of One's Soul
  • Seeking Union with the Holy One

✦ The Seeker can find the paths of the search embedded within:
  • Meditation
  • Concentration
  • Imagination
  • Receptivity
  • Sacrifice
  • Mysticism

Seekers form a philosophy and way of living through a variety of spiritual practices:

✦ Eastern (Hinduism and others) seek to get off the karmic wheel, and therefore off the Earth cycle. This is the seeking of Spirit and separating Spirit from Matter.

- ✦ Western (Judaism, Christianity, and Egyptology) seek to be "of the world, but not in it," thus allowing the freedom of consciousness to be at rest, perceiving the Divine Energy as inherent in matter as well as in Spirit.

- ✦ Indigenous (Native American, Celtic, African, Aborigine, and others) seek to know Source by Union with Nature. They seek to become One with All in order to know Oneness. They believe Spirit and Matter are One. They do not seek to be out of this world. They seek to know Spirit, Live Spirit and Be Spirit in the Now.

We live the power and the order of this pathway through the Universal Law of Contraction and Expansion imprinted on this path of the Tree; thus, within the branches of our own consciousness. This Law provides two parts of a whole that are to be individualized (duality) – for instance, Source and Soul, non-matter and matter. It also presents the power of polarity, the opposing and complimentary energy that creates the arching of light that supports creation and manifestation.

This Law supports the vibration that whatever is within must come out and what is out must come in. Contraction provides the power to come within, listen to the Higher Wisdom, transform what has been experienced and expand out again. This expansion provides a new form, and an ability to depict and live at yet another level of the Whole. In order to understand and define this law within our lives, we must look at the powers of contraction and expansion to "grasp" the wisdom.

◆ The Universe is a constant motion of contraction and expansion:

- Moving in and moving out
- Involution and evolution
- Dark and light
- Spirit and matter
- Expressing and transforming
- Moon light and Sun light
- Sunset and sunrise
- Cycles and phases
- Inspiration and opportunity
- Wealth and poverty
- Destiny and chance
- Challenge and reward
- Beginning and ending
- Black and white

Contained within the essence of this Law is a view of life. We all learn

◆ Everything has a cycle, a season unto itself

◆ Every cycle and every season lives, grows, dies, and rebirths (spiral)

◆ Harmonizing comes when one honors this law without getting stuck in the fears of change and the need to hold on to what was (circle)

When this quality of consciousness is understood through our mind, emotions, ego and physical realities, we create an understanding and a union with the Whole. We know that there is a sequence or evolution of life that allows us to explore and experience it all. Thus, we continue our soul quest and journey toward the point of Manifestation. Taking in the next Sphere of Source Consciousness, we learn more of the process of the Universe and recognize our own processing as we live the Tree of Life.

SPHERE 5 – SEVERITY

A blazing swirl of Red light reveals another vortex of Universal Consciousness. It is named *Severity* and holds good cause for such a name. This mass of light swirls and is the central sphere on the Pillar of Form that emanates the vibration of Love from the Holy Mother to Her Child. It is the sphere of consciousness that tears down, breaks apart and purifies (remember when Mom asked you to clean your room?). It is the pattern of consciousness intended to create the most perfect outcome.

As you are creating what you *really, really, really* want; think of yourself as an artist who is perfecting your outcome. You have painted a picture of the reality and know you carry from the Sphere of Mercy, every talent, ability to manifest, and tools needed to succeed. Now in this sphere, you are reviewing your creation and making sure you have succinctly designed it. As you ponder this, you have an opportunity to change the design, reset the matrix of intention and clear anything from the design that will not work for what you really want.

Take some time to contemplate the meaning of this from the Higher, Monadic, state of consciousness. What is the Divine doing? It has created the individuated state of existence through the agency of Souls. It has provided everything that is to be needed, desired, used, experienced and explored, through the agency of the Sphere of Mercy. And now, it is tearing it down? Breaking it apart? Is it preparing the kiln of life to perfect the outcome? Meditate on this concept!

This is, by far, one of the most interesting spheres on the Living Tree of Life. It carries the energy of breaking down, clearing, ending and new beginnings. It is the hell of Transformation, yet the heaven of Healing. It is a doorway of Life and a doorway of Death. It is the powerful containment of chaos (Sphere of Wisdom), yet in a new way as it has embraced the wisdom and activity of the Spheres of Understanding and Mercy. It is the carrier of the Ideation of the Creator. The perfect archetypal designs in the Imagination of the Supernal Triad are preparing to be sculptured and crystallized for use by the individual soul. These will be refined and re-sculptured to mold and fit into the realm of manifestation. This is a fiery sphere, so you might think of it as the kiln of the clay maker, preparing to establish the final design. Remember the clay maker must make sure the temperature is correct or the clay will dry and crumble and be no more.

Heat is passion, purpose, will power and the intense drive to fulfill desires. All of this is necessary to carry a dream to the fruition of manifestation. Note these levels within yourself as you continue to design your plan to manifest what you truly want. As you can see, Severity is the polarity of Mercy. Severity brings the form of truth and the strengthening of the intellect into the mixture of the life substance flowing through the consciousness of the individual in the Higher Self Triad.

The Individual is the offspring of Source, whose purpose is to evolve through the experiences of manifestation as the endowment of the Holy Trinity is bestowed upon them. The Sphere of Beauty represents the offspring, while Mercy and Severity represent the duality of the Higher-Self expressed in Beauty.

The three-level state of consciousness, represented in the Higher-Self Triad, does not descend into the lower frequencies. It is only found by the individual via raising consciousness to the higher dimension of self. This point of reference most definitely reminds us of the importance to meditate, expand our consciousness and realize we are more than what we see in this Earthly existence. It calls us to recognize that we vibrate at a denser frequency in the physical form.

Though there is nothing wrong with this dense reality, it carries a challenge of not realizing we are more than Earthly experiences. We can raise our vibration and realize our spiritual qualities by expanding and aligning with the higher ratio of awareness that is contained within our unconscious qualities of our higher self. We must enter the chambers of inner awareness and slip through the veils of consciousness that contain the vibrations of higher frequencies.

Radical Intelligence, an ability to proceed from the Root of Source, exudes from this whirling sphere of consciousness. The energy of Source (the Crown) flows through the path of Expression wells up in the Sphere of Understanding, overflows into the path of containment and spills into the Sphere of Severity. The ultimate patterns of manifestation held in the Sphere of Understanding are released into Creative Ideation (Sphere 5, Severity) for existence in the world of matter to occur.

The power of the Divine Emanating into the Soul-Child provides the Soul-Child with Authority of its world (lower seven spheres of consciousness). This power provides Perfect Desire through Mercy and Perfect Truth through Severity, activated through the Soul of the Higher-Self.

The catabolic power of Severity is a higher order of destructive energy. The dissolution releases energy which is used for a new construction (or creative ideation). It provides power to determine a new form and a new life-cycle. When form can no longer hold the force, it must dissolve, releasing the force, and shape-shift into a new form. Though Severity appears to act forceful, it is not force – it is the active use of force. Mercy is the Force and the fuel. Severity is the Lamp – both are needed to create the light. Force and Form; Act and Contain.

Severity is the Containment of Force. It is not cruel, but can be painful if the limitations of a particular form are not accepted. We often see this happen when we are not willing to follow through and complete something that has long been done in our lives.

+ The perpetual student who will not leave school and achieve a career status.

+ A relationship that has done its service and now, complete, is painfully held together.

+ A job that cannot serve creative expression is clung to because of fear of financial loss or other losses.

This holding on becomes the unanswerable pain experienced when one tries to achieve a new position, a new point of creativity in their life, but nothing seems to happen. The release has not occurred from the past and the new cannot be recognized.

This sphere of consciousness brings the strength and courage used to create, manifest and release. Through the power of faith, and the expression of unconditional love, this sphere provides the ability to move through the time of contained manifestation until one is done with the process and released and set free the energy so it may transform into a new reality. The power of assessment must be brought to bear in order to help make the change.

Judgment is another name of Severity. It is what helps make the changes. Its most succinct meaning provides an awareness that judgment is:

+ The Power of Assessment

+ Used to indicate the power to determine how the creative energy of Mercy is used

+ Related to Intuition (inner ability to discern Truth)

+ An alignment with Your Truth and Divine Truth (not everyone else's)

+ Truth on the creative level is perfection

+ Truth must be strong in order to contain Force – otherwise, the creative force falls to the wayside as wasted energy

The form and experiences produced by the Sphere of Severity are temporary. When purpose is achieved, this state of consciousness allows them to die. Regeneration occurs, releasing new energy; for in this point of consciousness, new forms can be created. This can be the death of an event, idea, relationship, human, cell or universe. Death results when force breaks through and destroys the vehicle, which can no longer contain the form and a new vehicle must be developed for the new stages of creation.

Severity holds the power of protection that is enforced by Source. The experience of breaking down also is the ability to release whatever is detrimental to the growth of your soul. That which is detrimental is severed from your experience through the agency of this sphere of consciousness. Before it is released, you move through many cycles that help you learn discipline, develop strength, live courageously and master qualities that provide the gateway to the unlimited bounty of Mercy and Success. You develop the power to change as you cycle through this sphere of consciousness and you realize:

✦ Change is necessary for the growth of the Universe as well as the Individual

✦ Judgment is used to ascertain how long a particular pattern should last (pattern of experiences, lifestyles, relationships, jobs, creative endeavors, etc.)

✦ Whenever something ceases to be beneficial to growth, it signals the need for dissolution

✦ Whatever is conducive to one's growth, will continue

Often an individual's greatest fear is change. Without change, static energy:

✦ Keeps one in immature childhood rather than mature development

✦ Keeps one clinging to the old because they cannot see the new. This limits faith and causes fear that he might be left with nothing

In truth, what one might be saving is nothing. It is dying because it is useless. If someone tries to maintain what is dying, they will suffer the painful burns from the fire of dissolution. If one is willing to transform, they will find that change is the Power of Sacrifice for a higher good. At this point, one is at a state of surrender.

✦ Surrender for the sake of something of a Higher Priority

✦ Surrender is to give way to the changing force and allow a new creation to be released

✦ Surrender allows the "let go" process to release the mind and emotions from restriction to enter into dissolution to establish a new form

Mercy and Severity reveal that the power of Source is constructive and destructive. To become like the Divine Parents, we must understand that Source makes decisions, is responsible for these decisions, is not afraid to destroy experiences that outlive usefulness and create newness repetitively, cyclically and without judgment of Right or Wrong. It simply IS. To live in this state of awareness calls us to live the virtues of this sphere, which are Energy and Courage.

✦ Energy pushes, drives and shatters crystallization that is no longer useful

✦ Courage defends, even in the process of destruction

✦ Both Energy and Courage are essential processes of life

Of course, where there is a virtue, there is a vice and this sphere reveals the vices of Cruelty and excessive Destruction. Cruelty can occur on all levels. At higher levels, there is more pain and it lasts longer. Excessive destruction comes when valuable and productive energy that could still be used is destroyed, but fear has overcome the personality and a willingness to persevere is lost in the need to hold onto what is not useful.

Archangel Khamael holds the matrix and intent of this

Sphere. She is the caretaker of the dissolution process and the purification resulting from the action. She encourages the enthusiasm and zeal of the true believer, supporting the desires of transformation.

Archangel Khamael is also known as an 'Angel of Death.' She helps dissolve and release the past, the fears, and the negative judgments that may be held. She is certainly known as an angel who helps in the transit from Earthly life to spiritual essence when the physical body dies. However, as an agent in support of your quest to manifest, she will be by your side to help you discover your strength, use your courage and comprehend the integrity of your higher-self. She will help you live with humility, which is the knowing that you are a part of the Whole as is everyone, and all parts are necessary to establish your individual qualities. In such a state, you will be merciful with others, as well as yourself. You will use the power of love to release and regenerate new states of existence.

Khamael will help you know how far you can go on your Journey of Life. If you are moving into territories that you are not ready to experience, Khamael will send you signals, throw up road blocks and remind you of the territory you are about to enter. This is often experienced as life experiences that seem to get in the way of what you want to manifest. Take time to reassess and understand if you have everything in alignment for the new level. Have you let go of the past? Have you released emotional ties that hinder you? Have you matured enough to understand how to handle the new position of your desire?

Khamael is a guardian and protector of the Soul, and will always be there to support your growth and indicate when you are about to set yourself up for a course in life that is more painful than you need to experience. Like all angelic beings, she will not interfere with your Free Will and Choice. She will attempt to bring thought-forms and feelings through to suggest a better way or encourage awareness of the challenging lessons you are about to enter and explore.

Khamael can be quite severe in insuring the safety of the soul – her ultimate goal is to serve Source. If the soul is not ready to be purified to mingle with Source and create as Source does, Khamael will step in and tweak consciousness so the higher growth can occur (even if it requires going back to Step One on the Path of Evolution). You might compare this state of consciousness with the Mother who is firm enough to guide her children down a path of life that will benefit them, even if they cannot see the benefit in their moment of immaturity. From the standpoint of using this exercise to manifest your desires, if you are unable to handle the heat of transformation, Khamael will send the vibrations necessary to stop the waste of time and energy and lead you down a path of education and maturity so you can be ready to manifest a clean and concise outcome of your desire.

To help you use the power of the Sphere of Severity and the assistance of Khamael, the pathways are lit and energy is there for you to follow. Review the Path of Self-Dominion. For in this sphere, energy has been blended with the Sphere of Mercy to assist in individual growth through the Sphere of Severity.

PATH OF INSTRUCTION

Emanating from Severity, a welcoming emerald light glows on this path. It welcomes the ability to be instructed by your Higher-Self so you may learn how to continue your journey into manifestation. In fact, this path connects Severity to Beauty (the focal point of this triad). From the Pillar of Form and the Sphere of Severity, lessons of containment continue to assist. Containment at the spiritual level is the holding, blending and weaving together of energy that will be used to manifest anything. Containment is a gift on a personal level for knowing how to set the parameters of your life. It is a knowing of what you can do and what you cannot do right now. It is a gift for creating the right balance so manifestation of what you *really* want can occur. To be willing to be instructed provides you with the power to know how to create with the knowing you are a creator.

This pathway calls forward the Intelligence of Faith. True Faith provides the awareness that all you know resides within you and beyond you and within Source. Whenever you supplicate the Universal Presence for answers, manifestations, healing and all that you need, you indicate your faith by using the following words "Amen," or "So Be It." You release the power to make the prayer firm and establish what you know into the realm of matter. You hold steadfast to the reality that you are instructed along the way to manifest, step-by-step, anything that is needed to build the final desire into the realm of materialization.

At the moment, you use the term "Amen" or "So Be It,' you release the *Primal Mover,* the Source of motivational impulses encoded within that allows all things to proceed. The encoded power within you honors that which Is, Was, and Always Will Be. It calls you to work with the knowledge within and without, particularly intuitive knowledge, so you may "hear the voice of faith" and respond to it.

Your response is both inward and outward. Your inner

feelings and beliefs will shape-shift, mold the clay, if you will, and temper the outcome. Outwardly, your actions will assist the development of the outcome as well. As discussed in the Path of Mastery emanating from the Supernal Triad, you must have at least 2/3^{rds} of your consciousness vibrating with a positive knowing – *faith* – for the true outcome to occur.

As is known from the wisdom of the Tree of Life, everything that is needed to proceed in life is already encoded within your soul. To learn how to manifest, the Law of Cause and Effect is always moving through your inner and outer awareness. It reminds you that what you think and feel is what is used to manifest an outcome. This path holds this Law in place for your Higher Self, Personal Self and all existence to use. To achieve what you want, it is important that you know this Law and how you use it within your conscious and unconscious reality. This Law tells us that for every action, there is an equal and opposite reaction. For every thought, there is a response. For every feeling, there is an equal force reflected back. When there is one thing, there is another; such as:

- ✦ If there is light, there is dark
- ✦ If there is a head, there is a tail
- ✦ If there is black, there is white
- ✦ If there is red, there is green
- ✦ If there is soft, there is rough
- ✦ If there is an entrance, there is an exit
- ✦ If there is birth, there is death
- ✦ If there is death, there is birth

This is also known as the Law of Karma. "Karma" translates to "action" or "work." It is a reminder that every action you take will yield an equal reaction. It is the Golden Rule we all grew up with – "Do unto others as you would do unto you." It is the law that calls you to understand that what you put out, you will get back; what you sow, you will reap.

On this bough of the Tree, you are called to be clearly aware of what you are reaping at all levels of yourself. In reaping, you can tell where your mind and feelings have truly been focused. What you reap reveals your balance or imbalance in several areas of your life:

- Self	- Soul Self - Higher Self
- Money	- Values
- Communication	- Education
- Family	- Benevolent Acts
- Creativity	- Innovation
- Service	- Health
- Relationships	- Intimacy
- Sharing	- Investing
- Spiritual Practice	- Philanthropy
- Career	- Outer Expression
- Groups of People	- Friends
- Sacred Living	- Mysteries to resolve

As you review the Living Tree of Life, you can see how your life and the Universe have moved into and out of polarities, balance and imbalance, and the awareness and shadows of existence. It simply is the way of life and the more you realize it; the more you can take charge of the ins and outs, the ups and downs by being more at the level of Cause rather than Effect. You will direct the course of your desires, for you are given the right to do that at the very moment individuation took place and the Laws of the Universe were automatically encoded into every soul.

You may think you are only at the Effect side of the Law, but you are not. You are given a mind to think with, feelings to create with and a physical world to manifest your desires into useable form. You are to learn, as this path teaches, that you have the ability to know what you want, have faith that you have everything you need to accomplish what you want, and to put it into action with your thinking, feeling and acting at the causal level. Here, you are at the point of brewing just the right T.E.A.

Make a note and reveal to yourself how your thoughts, emotions, and actions support the desires you wish manifested in your daily reality. Check out your inner truth – is it congruent with what you want or is it congruent with what you fear? The Law of Cause and Effect is automatic and it will form the outcome based on your strongest reality.

PATH OF REVERSE AND REFLECT

This bough on the Tree exudes blessings from the Sphere of Severity and holds many secrets of the Universe in action. It continues to reveal how you use the vibrations of Source. It is at this point that awareness is stirred to realize that Source has reversed its undivided self into individuated pieces (souls). It is also at this point that the reversal allows Source energy to be contained and used by the individual. The reflection of Source is a constant in the cells of every soul.

This path carries the color of ocean blue. Are you coloring your Pathways and Spheres in the illustration? Are you writing in the names of the Spheres and Pathways? This will help your inner psyche release the wisdom that you already have and move the intuitive knowledge to your cognitive awareness.

The mystery of this path is not only the power of Source reversing Itself, but that it is a stabilizing intelligence called the 'Ocean of Consciousness.' Is this an oxymoron? Perhaps. It is not about the movement of the ocean of water we are so familiar with, but the Great Womb of Containment that allows awareness and stabilization of the Creative Force and the ability to birth this force into a material reality.

In Esoteric philosophy, it is known by the masters that the Spirit of the Mighty Waters is the most stable. The masters recognize that the Ocean of Consciousness is the First Principle in alchemy that underlies everything else. The water of the Great Womb is the primordial element. It stabilizes us until we are developed enough to emerge as the Creators that we are. This bough on the Tree is the Life giving energy of the Divine Mother flowing through our Higher Self. To know this wisdom, we must reverse the trends of our human beliefs and transform into the Light that we are.

Of course, Laws of the Universe help us and this path actually carries a Dual Law – The Law of Reversal and the Law of Reflection. The Law of Reversal indicates that a full 180 degree turnabout occurred at the point the Universe released itself into individual soul qualities. At that very moment, every soul took on the power to reverse any aspect of itself as well. The turnabout allows evolution of denser emanations of light to express higher emanations of light by changing consciousness. We use it best when we:

- ✦ Reverse the tendencies of thought, word and action that contain us in an ostentatious view of our own life limiting the view of the higher mind and higher intent contained within

- Trends of Thoughts
- Trends of Emotions
- Trends of Actions
- Trends of Interactions
- Trends of Health
- Trends of Lack
- Trends of Self-Inflicted Negativity and Self-Inflicted Punishment

This Law asks that you look at your life and the areas you may need to reverse and take charge to reverse those areas. Each day, there is something that will happen that you may need to transform into a higher state and live your life according to your higher message within. Always search for Truth, the way and the means to live at that higher level and you will reverse any challenges that seem to hold you in the negative aspects of living. When you do this, you allow the full power of the positive energy of the Law of Reflection, the second law on this path.

The Law of Reflection simply states that the angle of reflection always equals the angle of incidence. It is quite similar to the Law of Cause and Effect. However, it allows you to look at the trends in your life and recognize that they are a reflection of what is happening within your inner self. When you reverse your lower trends of feeling, thinking and acting, you will reflect the Source within and think, feel and act as Source. Your Search for Truth will cause you to reflect the Higher Wisdom in and through you. What do you see in your life now that reflects Source?

The gift of this bough on the Tree, the Spheres of Mercy and Severity and all other pathways of light you have explored, prepare you for the Neutral Pillar and central point on the Tree of Life. This is the Heart of the Tree and the Sphere called **Beauty.** It is the contained field of energy of the Higher Self of Humanity. Within you, it is your own Higher Self and the perfectly balanced state of your essential essence.

SPHERE 6 - BEAUTY

A brilliant gold-yellow light beams from the Heart of the Tree and the central point of your Higher-Self. The Sphere of Beauty is the focal point of the Higher-Self Triad. All energy flows from above to this sphere and all energy flows from it to the manifesting point of the lower spheres. In truth, energy flows from above to below and below to above with this sphere being the central and harmonizing point of all energy of the Tree of Life.

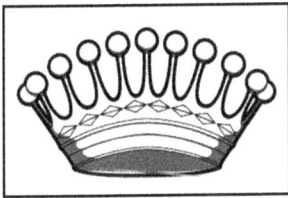

This vortex, called 'Beauty,' is the Throne of the Children of Source. The Crown descends and is placed on the Head of All. Every child inherits the Will Power of Source at this point. This vortex of consciousness is only comprehended when we align with our higher-self and not simply believe that our Earthly reality is the only reality that we exist within.

The following quote from the _Holy Bible_ describes the Light and Power of this Sphere of Consciousness.

"The Word was in the beginning, and that very Word was with God, and God was that Word. The same was in the beginning with God. Everything came to be by

his hand; and without him not even one thing was created came to be. The life in Him and the life is the light
of men. And the same light shines in darkness, and the
darkness does not overcome it."

—*Gospel According to St John – Chapter 1, Verses 1:5*

The Living Tree of Life reveals that the Light shines within each individual. At this Sphere of Beauty, consciousness
is represented as the Higher-Self of humans, collectively and
personally. It is noted that individuals who develop the awareness of this Light have the power to reign over the Kingdom
(the Earthly existence). Light is considered Ultimate Awareness. It is the empowerment of the Creative Experience.

Light or Awareness, is also called the Expression of Right
Mediation – the point of integrating All Energies and thus
balancing and harmonizing lower frequencies with higher
frequencies. All energies of the spheres surrounding this
sphere of consciousness are multiplied by the union and empowered by the Light, Life and Will of The Ultimate Soul-
Child, the Christ Consciousness, and the Higher-Self within.

This point of the Living Tree is the Hub of the Wheel of
Life. It holds all other points of consciousness in balance so
the wheel turns smoothly and evenly. It is the continuous
movement of Source. It equalizes all forces of consciousness,
stabilizes and balances their forms, and holds the projection
of Source that is used as all aspects of existence.

Take a moment to realize what this means to you and your
alignment with the intent to manifest your desires. This state
of consciousness is where you integrate your personal self
(lower or denser energy) with your Higher-Self. Your Earthly
desires, mixed with this sphere of light, take on the presence
of Source's intent to manifest. Your union with this Point

of Consciousness harmonizes your desire with the upper regions of awareness and energy fields of creativity to bring you to the wheel of life ready to turn and manifest your dreams into a human reality. What it requires of you is to be still in the Center Point and allow the mixture of your dreams and desires to integrate with the highest element of Consciousness, coagulate through the weaving of higher mind, higher heart and higher frequencies of perfection. As you allow this to occur, you take on the power of inheriting and gain all that has been bequeathed to you.

As the Soul-Child, you inherit the Countenance of Source and through advancement of consciousness, you gain the power of the Vast Countenance. You also leave an imprint of wisdom for successive generations to receive and use. The great potential of the Universal inheritance is left to them to manifest the Gold of the Universe. As the indigenous people always share, it is important to reach and live from your Highest Potential and realize it is the legacy to be used by the next seven generations after you. **You always leave a legacy.**

Your connection to this sphere aligns you with The Omniscient One – The All-Knowing Creator. From this state of being is released Infinite Awareness through you. It liberates within you the Will to Create. The energy of balance and harmony leaves you with the highest level of awareness and faith. The integration of faith and awareness creates Knowing and in Knowing is the realization that all is in perfect order within this Universe (no matter how it looks personally), and therefore within you. When this Knowing occurs, you become a full-time active creator with the Divine and in your role as Co-Executive, take dominion over your world.

To gain this knowing requires a sacrifice from you. Sacrifice the beliefs that you are only a Human Being. Sacrifice the beliefs that this world you live in is the dictator of life events. Let go of the beliefs that you are a victim of circumstances dictated by your family, education, relationships, health or any other false perception that human beliefs seem to hold. Sacrifice S.I.N. (Self Inflicted Negativity). Move into the virtue of this sphere, which is Devotion, and you will find your perfect center point – your Inner Heart. This point will help you sacrifice the attitudes, beliefs and actions that keep you from your Higher-Self.

Of course, be devoted to the Highest Source of life. Allow yourself to be completely dedicated to the higher principles of life. Live with the attitude that All Life Matters. Allow yourself to be governed by spiritual principles in every area of your existence. For in so doing, nothing will be kept from you. Your desires easily come into manifested realities. What you *really, really, really* want easily forms.

Temperance is called for and on this path. If temperance is not adhered to, the shadow of this sphere occurs as a vice in your life. This vice is Arrogance and lower levels of Pride. Such states create separation from higher awareness and all people, circumstances and events in your life. Arrogance is a state of consciousness stirred by fear that you cannot be seen as important and must display arrogance in order to be recognized as an important being. Arrogance is a form of Pride that requires you to compare yourself to others, which always leaves you falling a bit short from the act of judgment that has been used. Rather than recognizing your Higher-Self and ability to achieve, you will only use external fulfillment to prove you are okay. Most generally, you always see someone doing better than you. Comparison is a dark corner of energy stirring low self-esteem.

Harmony, peace and balance create the way back to your

Center Point. From your Center Point, you will live from your Higher Intent and realize that you are inheriting everything you need to fulfill your life dreams. From a healthy ego, vivacious self-esteem emerges from the Center Point, the Sphere of Beauty on the Living Tree of Life.

Out of this matrix of consciousness, Archangel Michael assists. Righting the imbalances, creating harmony out of disharmony and bringing chaos into its creative process of design and fulfillment is his action for Source. This 'Prince of Light,' as Archangel Michael is called, is directed to keep all forces moving in rhythm and balance. He is called to hold the Single Source in a cohesive state in the minds and hearts of all beings. He governs the distribution of all the energies into the manifest world.

This agent of Source helps heal emotional wounds so every individual may connect with the Higher-Self within. He teaches individuals how to harmonize and reach the masterful level they can achieve. He reveals that the Power of Love is the one true source that will heal, balance and create harmony in all levels of existence.

At the level of shaping and designing the final outcome to be manifest, Archangel Michael calls you to love every step, know you are Divinity expressing through the theater of human life, and radiate your Light to the world. He calls you to seek balance by living and expressing from the Heart of the Living Tree. It is he who will help you learn to transform, temper and know that you are living on all levels of the Universe at once and carry all possibilities within you. He will help you decipher and use the boughs on the tree that extend Light from Beauty.

PATH OF TRANSFORMATION

The radiant light of crimson illuminates this Path. It is an inner emotional fire that yearns to transform from one state of consciousness to another. It is the urge within to manifest the desires that are passionately felt and uncontrollably emerging. This Light encourages the proliferation of all possibilities known at the Source level and experienced at the personal level. This bough on the tree extends downward to the triad of the individual Soul and rustles yet another Veil of Destiny. It is moving energy preparing for another transformation. From the ethereal state of consciousness, there is a pulse of desire ready to form in the realm of the human processes. Within yourself, that is felt like a deep urging to get to the outcome of your desire. Your drive, purposeful actions and deep passion is set free.

The path of transformation releases energy into the Sphere of Victory. This energy is a synthesis of energy from Above outpouring Below into the Soul Triad. Therefore, the energy of Knowing everything already IS is steady and streaming into the destiny of manifestation.

The crimson bough on the Living Tree of Life initiates a power of a process of synthesis that calls for the blending of five archetypes. To blend these five levels creates a union with the kingdom of the Higher-Self. It awakens the realization that each being is a Microcosm in the Macrocosmic Universe and each is the Macrocosm in the Microcosm. (This paradox can be discovered at the cellular level, intelligently and intuitively through meditation.) The Five States are:

- ✦ **Heal** – Heal beliefs that wound, then expand to higher regions of a Compassionate Love for All Life

- **Reverse** – Invert trends of thoughts from the limited reality of the 3rd dimension and reflect the True Power, True Reality and True Expression of your Higher-Self.

- **Connect** – Maintain a constant review of the connection with Divinity, Soul-Consciousness and the power to transform any level of being into the vibrations of Higher Energy/Higher Consciousness.

- **Speak** – Use the Power of Words to create the Reality you desire

  - Speak and Be

  - Speak only what you want

- **Transform** – Transformation means to end something. Know when to put an end to thoughts that no longer create a viable and vivified manifest, words that no longer speak the Truth and actions that no longer support the manifested desire.

The Universe in its magnificent wisdom releases the Law of Transformation on this Path. This Law expresses the potential to surrender that which is completed and trigger the movement of energy toward a higher state of existence. Climbing down the Tree indicates Source is releasing the Individual Soul, knowing Its Great Work can only be completed by the individual state of consciousness. This Law indicates that a birth occurs at a new vibratory alignment and that which has been hidden becomes the revealed. That which has been a dream becomes the manifest. No matter how we look at it, transformation is a constant reality in the ebb and flow of the Universe. Each day is a transforming day. We have an internal mechanism that calls us to transform, especially when the potential of one level has completed its cycle and must expand to new levels of expression. Only our fears and avoidances rebuke the new states and appear to create static living. Nothing is static, so we are only living in the aches and pains of the avoidance (false perceptions, frustrations, angers, judgment and false justification).

In the challenging state, we may think there is no change occurring, but change occurs nonetheless as nothing can remain the same (one day to the next, one hour to the next, even one minute to the next). On this path, we can surrender to the change or struggle with false beliefs held within our subconscious.

In the magical mysteries of the Universe, another bough on the Tree helps us release the beliefs, receive support and temper our realities so we transform and allow the continual evolution from nonmatter to matter to occur. The next path, Angelic Support, reveals this gift of consciousness.

PATH OF ANGELIC SUPPORT

There are many guardian angels supporting the journey of each soul. This path reveals the intent of Source to provide angelic assistance and the preparation to cross another Veil of Destiny as the Light emanates from the Sphere of Beauty to the Sphere of Foundation, which is the focal point in the Soul Triad.

As this bough on the tree is part of the Neutral Pillar, it causes pause to reflect and balance, so integration can occur. It carries an intelligence that is called 'Tentative' or 'Probationary.' This is a point of consciousness that a "testing" time occurs as the Soul prepares to cross into the lower triads. This testing helps transform and transmute the Power of Light into the Temple of the Personality. It also provides a testing for the personality so we may walk in the light and express the light of our Higher-Self. This pathway provides us the angelic assistance for working with this intelligence.

There is a constant reminder that we never walk alone. The Light of the Divine is multi-faceted and on this path reveals itself in the multiple realities of angelic beings supporting every need. According to the wisdom of the Tree of Life, angels are the guardians of the Matrix of All Things Created by Source. They are Source and in Oneness they are States of Consciousness, we access as individualistic Vibrations of a Higher Order. They are:

+ Messengers of Source

+ Guardians of Individuals and Experiences

+ Overseers of Groups

+ Helpers of all areas of our lives

+ Record Keepers of the Aeons of Time

With this knowledge, pause for a moment and recant in your mind and heart what you are preparing to manifest. A truth exists that everything already IS. That desire is already a completely formed Matrix in Source Consciousness. You have been urged to develop it in the land of matter. A guardian holds the Matrix, waiting for you to connect with the desire and the drive to bring it to fruition. You do not have to know the name of the angelic assistant. You can simply call it the angel of whatever it is you are trying to manifest.

For instance, are you attempting to bring forth a career in the healing arts? Call on the Angel of Healing Careers. Do you know if you want to be a surgeon? Then, call on the Angel of Surgeons. Are you wishing to bring forth a desired relationship? Call on the Angel of Relationships. Is there a particular relationship you are feeling a desire to manifest? Is it a friendship, a marriage, a group or community relationship? Call on the specific angel of the relationship that you want to manifest. Angels will respond to your call. You only need to ask.

As you continue to live through this path, the currents and cycles of life are felt and the higher intelligence for tempering and keeping all in balance occurs. Probing and searching for an understanding of how to use Universal Power occurs before acting out desires in the world of manifestation. You learn to control your natural energies and take dominion of your desires by using the higher order of consciousness. You test your beliefs and temper your ability to adjust, transform and release old beliefs that do not acknowledge or allow the higher order to move into the realm of matter. You verify what truly works. At times, this comes through trial and error until you skillfully achieve what you want.

This testing field is akin to the World of Formulation. You can hone your thoughts, emotions and actions until the true manifest occurs. Or, you can live in old beliefs and formulate incongruent realities and distort or abort your manifest. Probing your own intelligence and creating the trial and error for learning is often challenging and this Path is given the notation of "The Dark Night of the Soul." Meaning, you come into yet another vestige of your shadow and it seems like forever before you meet the Light of your Soul. However, when you are cognitive of what you are doing and addressing the inner challenges with a knowing that you truly cannot be bereft of your desires, then you move to the Light and the answers to resolve and release the old beliefs and allow the truer Will of Higher Purpose come forward.

Your ability to adapt to this changing form of consciousness allows you to grow and evolve. You have the ability to master your reality without a structured road map. You live from the inner knowing that you are shaping the outcome with your thoughts and feelings in a congruent alignment with the higher qualities of consciousness. The Law of Adaptation moves through this Path of Light and supports your ability to continually make the changes necessary to form the final outcome with perfected intent.

The Law of Adaptation provides the wisdom of awareness and the energy that allows changes to occur where an organism becomes better suited to the environment of its existence. The dream adapts to the energy of influence that determines the final structure and material pattern of matter. This Law teaches that every level of consciousness must adapt to its cause, form and function. Due to the power of evolution, this cause, form and function changes as each level of consciousness expands awareness and creates the natural need to adapt as a result.

Passive and Active realities exist in adaptation. One must be passive to acquire information for the change (i.e., listening from within) and then become active to achieve form and function. Spiritual cells become human cells. When the power of adaptation occurs (passive and active union) an alchemical event takes place. The alchemical moment destroys the old information and new experiences supersede the old. At the spiritual, emotional and personal level, we experience our "Ah Ha!" moment or have an epiphany (a moment of sudden and great revelation). We are comfortable in knowing that all is in perfect order. We *know* our desires and dreams will materialize. No doubt exists. Something more happens within. The alchemical process causes:

- Our awareness to turn to a Higher Point of Reference
- Our intentions turn to Higher Purpose
- Our life turns to Service
- Service to the Divine
- Service to our Higher-Self
- Service to Others
- Service in Love, Compassion and Understanding

A gift comes from this process of adaptation. It is the gift of creative qualities that manages energy within us and around us. It is the gift of love, graciousness and living in the Light of Truth. We recognize that we are living on all levels at all times and the Light of the next descending path is activated within us.

PATH OF LIVING

This bough on the tree radiates the color of deep blue violet (indigo). Emanating from the Heart of the Tree, this light provides a stable branch of consciousness that helps the continuance of opening the Veil of Destiny once more. When lifted, this veil provides the flow and consciousness to manifest the Original Idea of Source and the original idea of your dreams into the realm of matter.

Stepping across a veil of consciousness is a very important concept to understand. It provides a new force and flow of energy moving through our consciousness. It provides the moment to renew our vows of intent to achieve. At a higher level, it calls us to Higher Intentful Living.

Intentful Living calls us to rise to the awareness of how

to live more like the Source we contemplate, rather than the Collective Awareness of the 3rd Dimension. It calls us to mastery through requiring awareness that we are responsible for our thoughts, feelings and actions at greater levels than before (every step advances every level of our being). It calls all of us to be ever aware of our illusions of being separate, or that our life is the result of what others "do to us or say to us." It calls us to be aware of how we believe others live their lives might influence our personal outcome. If we are not willing to move along the lines of the Higher Intent, we will only fool our self into believing that we cross the veil, yet only live as we think others want us to live rather than the Source Center Living we are intended to express.

When we are in illusion, we turn to the judgment of others and call on our ego to support this falsehood to help us survive using outmoded beliefs and attitudes. In fact, we continue living at a poverty level where our:

+ Love is false concern for others, from others, for our self – and even for Source (when would Source need our concern?)

+ Energy to live healthy dissipates

+ Creative ideas are not tapped

+ Connective power to the Is-ness is lacking

+ Financial abundance is in the ozone of possibilities with no result

+ All forms of abundance are in the ozone of possibilities with no results

To move out of this condition of a limited view of life, we have to allow our inner eye to become the vision capable of seeing through the Eye of Source. While viewing only through the personal eye, the mysteries and truth of life are hidden. When seeing life through the Eye of Source, we can view life beyond appearances. We no longer create illusion and live by false perception. We stop deceiving ourselves. We adjust our vision and see from the bigger picture of life, the vision of our Soul and the vision of Source. This adjusted vision allows us to see the ultimate truth of experiences, and helps us focus and achieve what we ultimately want to manifest. The adjusted view renews our intelligence and expands our awareness that everything is capable of renovation or transformation and can be renewed at any point on the journey to manifest.

When our human concepts can adjust and renew our intelligence to a higher order, false perceptions, false pretenses and false beliefs can be left in the roots of transformation. Then, we experience refreshingly new viewpoints of Source, of life experiences, and most certainly different views of our self and others. We recognize that we are living at multiple levels of experiences; not just the human experience.

The Law of Living, which reveals that we are living in multiple dimensions, is activated on this bough of the Tree. As we climb through this state of consciousness, we are aware of this activation within our individual selves. We feel, know and act from more than one dimensional awareness and recognize how we exist beyond our personal perceptions. On this Path, if we live with one eye open and one eye closed, we believe only in limited realities. Or, we can open our eyes to the Greater Truth and Greater Wisdom and live fully, moment-by-moment, aligned with a more complete awareness of our Inner and True Power.

Dimensions of consciousness include our personal reality, our subconscious reality, the collective unconscious of our

Earthly tribe, the automatic consciousness of the Universe, and the total and complete consciousness of the Divine. Our dimensions are filled with matter and non-matter and can be described in the following manner:

First Dimension – In the first dimension, a deep and wonderful mystery is held. It is the Mystery of the One and the Many and the Many and the One. It begins with Source. The energy is a single point of light. Contained within this single point is Everything that exists, will exist and has existed. Source vertically extends Its light beam on a single ray to radiate its Wholeness into individual expression.

The First Dimension, as it is known to our world, is a straight line moving within itself. It is a single dimension and a length that is measured, but not arcing. From the Essence of Source, it is the Single Point of Light expressing itself. It is the extension of a linear measurement that becomes a time line for aeons, epochs and eras. Of course, One Dimension, in spiritual terms presents the powerful awareness that we are One Dimensional – we are Spirit. At the human level, one dimension is a simple basic energy field.

Second Dimension – Energy in motion at the 2nd Dimension reveals that the singular energy moving forward and backward, up and down, and even sideways, creates arcing vibrations and intersections as a field of energy moves in a direction beyond its own linear alignment. Then, it generates a curve forming a new length, expanding its width and fusing with an opposing length. At the point of fusion, an interaction is created that becomes both adherent and repulsive. The Second Dimension is a highly creative field of energy and begins to distribute the intent of the desired manifest of Source (and most certainly any desire of yourself). This molten energy stimulates the enrichment of our plane of existence (3rd Dimension) and through this ingenious process of the Divine, stimulates the soul's ability to express the same likeness and image of the Divine.

It is from this 2nd Dimensional Plane of consciousness that we work with the alchemical exchanges (Spirit-to-soul-to-matter; and/or intent-to-creative ideation-to-manifestation). The interdependence of each of the dimensions can be seen here. We need each level of consciousness vibrating and sending a resonant energy that continues the cohesiveness of the union with Source. In fact, there is a resounding resonance throughout the Universe that is the "connective tissue" of this cohesiveness.

Third Dimension – This Dimension holds the fields of touch, taste, hear, see and smell. It has depth and breadth. It is singular, yet multiple. It is complex, and yet simple. It is the expression of the paradox of Source. It is the place where polarities are "played out" in the Theater of Life. It extends itself up, down, around, in and out. It can be the dot, the line, an inanimate or an animate object. It is energy transformed to matter; and yet it contains non-matter (such as thoughts and emotions, ethereal levels of existence, molecules in motion, and so on).

This is the world of living, thinking and breathing. It is the expression of all you know from the wholeness of your being. It is your thoughts, feelings and action. It has seen parts and unseen realities of ethereal substances that form the dreams of your heart through the interweaving with the core of the Divine.

The Third Dimension is a world of choices. It is the 'yin'

and 'yang.' It is where you dance with polarities, swing with dichotomies and get lost in the unknown realties of time and space. It is the place where you can ignorantly walk for a lifetime without realizing that there is more than meets the eye, or where you can come to realize that the Universal fields of force and form are all about you, seen and unseen.

This Earth experience is your world to create within. Through the power of your thoughts and feelings, beliefs and knowing, you build the world around you. You create your reality and the dreams of your heart and soul-desires [that have emerged from the 1st and 2nd Dimensions). Look around, what have you created? Review what you really, really, really want to create. Become like the avatar that you are and form a focus of intent, spirit of purpose and alignment with the Divine to let Universal substance build the form of your dreams into the mold of human existence.

Fourth Dimension – It is in this dimension that you connect with the molecular, atomic, sub-atomic particles, such as quarks, and all minute qualities of the manifest world. You also have an entrance into the ethereal realities and make your connection with the intent of the Divine to manifest. In fact, it is from the words of the _Holy Bible_ that we hear of the power of the 4th dimension and the Power of Divine Sound, _"And the Word was Spoken, and the Word was Made Flesh."_ In the 4th Dimension, we are in touch with the Spiritual vibration of Sound and the power that Sound has in creating a manifest.

The 4th Dimension is definitely where you can feel the flow of molecules in action in a table, a car, a ball, a chair – all inanimate and animate expressions of Source. It is here where you discover that "everything" is alive. It is also here that you learn nothing is really solid. It is simply tremendous movement of energy that compacts the molecules of intent. It is that part of the ethereal world that is filled with thought formations from Divine Mind, Spiritual entities and Earth entities. It is a plane where the actual life forces interact and reach their concrete forms, both influential and causative. It is the cause of growth; the link between mind and matter. It is where your personal plan of an event is creatively built with ethereal substance for future materialization.

The 4th Dimension is the region of guardians that guide the human mind to greater levels of thinking and souls to ever expanding evolution. They guide and direct the path of any individual capable of asking for assistance. They help all beings as they traverse the world of unknowns (physical or spiritual). The guardians are angels, masters and wise souls who wish to help other souls on their path of upward, expanding consciousness.

__Fifth Dimension__ – This Dimension is a faster rate of vibration. This plane carries the imprint of Source in abstract forms that transfer into your Collective Consciousness (4th Dimension to 3rd Dimension). When you access it, the inspiration of Source initiates the communication of Itself through symbology. It is translated in your world through the processes of painting, writing, music, language of intuition, and all abstract realities. The inspiration is love-based. When you connect with this influence of love, you heal and create long-lasting healing at all levels of your existence. It is within the Fifth Dimension that you sense the spiral of light and leave the level of linear concepts and experiences. The power of love, joy, sensualness, clarity and excitation occur.

The greater complexities of building the planes of matter exist in the 5th Dimension. It is considered a level of consciousness where the building blocks that create intersections (matter and non-matter, polarity and duality) occur. The Fifth Dimension holds the power of abstract concepts that will become galaxies, planets and stars, people, animals, plants and stones, etc.

Sixth Dimension – During the descending process of the Tree of Life, this Dimension offers the passage of energy in which the necessity of using a soul-mind occurs (individuation). This provides a vehicle for the evolutionary cycle to initiate and the opportunity of "experiences" of Source to manifest. This is the Initiation of all aspects of life and purpose (reason for being a male or a female, being a bird or a fish, being a challenge or harmony; why empowerment or struggle, etc.).

Geometric formations occur in the 6th Dimension. In this Dimension, it is not just a beautiful art form – it is the matrix reality of Higher Purpose. The pure and perfect form of each individual essence is seen at this level. The vibrational frequency that triggers involution and evolution of Source is individualized at the Sixth Dimension and the code, geometric form, is released into existence.

Seventh Dimension – Men and Women adept in mystical wisdom long felt this was the highest dimension that could be reached. The Seventh Dimension has been considered the point of Nirvana – One with Source. They had not experienced the planes of reality that were tapped into by the ancient Egyptians, Mayans and the lost civilization called, the 'Anasazi,' the pre-pueblo people whose descendents are the Hopi, the Navajo and the Pueblo Indians. It is only in modern times that Shamans have been able to articulate more information of the dimensions ascending above the 7th. I believe this has occurred because our quantum scientists finally burst through the 4th and perhaps the 5th Dimensions and began to expound on the "new" powers that are now known to them (it is still necessary in our logical society that we must have scientists prove what ancients and modern Intuits have long known). It has been apparent that when a collective consciousness finally breaks through a dimensional reality, further dimensions open for discussion and articulation (fits the 100th Monkey theory).

Modern Intuits have cracked the veil and entered the land of the 7th Dimension and discovered it moves them into the greater cosmos. The vibrational waves that are experienced are a cosmic sound (we see this "sound" as light in brilliant white and color) and perhaps may be the sound of the angels, the Holy Living Creatures that are the light frequency directing us to remember we are the Pure Point of Source.

The 7th Dimension presents a place of peaceful feelings. However, it is also a place of a great magnitude of transformational energy. It is a point of consciousness in which the Divine Mind releases a lesser degree of its energy with the intent that Its plan to express through individuation can occur (to be a galaxy, a planet a star, air, gas, person, animal, plant, etc.). As we experience this energy, we undergo huge transitions in all arenas. It is an existence where the traumas of cataclysmic events are devoid of experience and harmony takes over on the biological, psychological, spiritual and cosmic levels. It is the place where the memory of only the Highest Purpose of our existence occurs. Yes, it is a Nirvana point, in that it presents the human consciousness the opportunity to live the Light of Source and explore the pathway of Peace. In this dimension, the DNA of all living matter is in its Perfect Order and Perfect Plan. Therefore, again, abiding in this dimension creates extraction of total healing qualities.

An increased power of Love is noted in the plane of the Seventh Dimension. Its vibrations flow through living organisms. This love creates the fine tuning within all nature to maintain its harmony, balance and perfect state of being. We sing, dance and soar when we are attuned by this vibration.

Eighth Dimension – Divine Mind is refined and experienced in the 8th Dimension. It is where meditators connect to the power of the Divine Mind and the Perfect Intent and Focus of a Higher Purpose. It is here the Light of Source is first known. This is where mystics indicate they have experienced a light that is blinding. It is also here that we might find people crossing over see the "blinding light," and feel they are being told it is not time for them to leave the Earthly existence yet.

The 8th Dimension is a converter of energy. It sends energy into the 7th Dimension where it is downloaded and decoded and sent on to the lower dimensions. It sends energy to the higher dimensions and decodes the experience held in the soul of the individual states.

Ninth Dimension – *As Above, So Below* reveals the essence of the Ninth Dimension. This dimension is a spinning, nucleus of Source sending forth Its vibrational intent to manifest. It will manifest in Time Waves (eras, epochs and eons). It is power existing outside of Earthly time, yet time derives from this Supreme Consciousness.

This energetic power of the Ninth Dimension continually receives the Force of Source as it passes through all other dimensions. The nature of this state of Source Consciousness is and creates various roles in the activity of universal evolution.

The 9th Dimension connects us to what the Native American medicine people, the Shamans of other indigenous cultures, and the Mystics call, *Great Mystery*. It contains within it the Power of the Force and the Form of the Great Creator (which is beyond explanation in our human language). Great Mystery is neither form nor force, neither male nor female, neither time nor space; and yet, Great Mystery is form and force, male and female, time and space and much more. We enter the domain of the Paradox as we capture the first level of the Dynamic Creator in the channel of the 9th Dimension.

In the Ninth Dimension, Present, Future and the Past exist (and yet no time exists). It is from this State of Consciousness, we can connect with the Soul's Past, Present and Future intent. It repeats the messages: We exist because of the Universe; the Universe exists because of us. To know the Universe, we must come within. The Universal canvas can only be found when we come within and find our soul position as Great Mystery artistically designing the whole picture through individuation.

Mystical Wisdom is decoded in this dimension... again it is Within. A high level of integration occurs on the personal level of an individual when aligning with the 9th Dimension. It also allows one to learn a new language that allows collective changes of soul-groups to meet Divine Intent.

Tenth Dimension – Ah, such energy the 9th Dimension provides. However, we are not done in our understanding of the dimensions. The 10th Dimension is a swirling light without boundaries. It is an infinite experience of all possibilities. Super String theorists believe this is the make up of the Universe in which we live. They put it akin to the 2nd Dimension where arching and energetic blasts create a movement into existence. Gaseous energies mixed with light extend the vibration of Source from the higher dimensions allowing the Tenth Dimension to begin the exploration into the super strings that will create millions, billions, trillions of "things" of the Universe. These things consist of what we know and see in the 3rd Dimension and more that we do not see, but know exist. We explore this realm of consciousness to enter into forms that will help build and rebuild the energies of healing and manifesting realities of a higher nature. This is an energy field that must be dealt with carefully and directly for in this Dimension, one can create havoc and blend thoughts and images into existence that are not of the original intent of healing. If one is not paying attention, a frequency of energy of "anything" can slip into the make up of intention and disturb the intended outcome.

Eleventh Dimension – Again, our quantum theorist brings us the language that helps us define the energies of higher consciousness. They connect the 11th Dimension with the M-Theory and make note that the 'M' stands for an array of concepts – Mother, Matrix, Membrane, Master, Magic, Mathematical (and offer the word Murky, just in case we are in the realm of illusion). But to our mystical awareness, the 11th Dimension and the Membrane are a perfect explanation of the experience of this dimension. In fact, I liken it to the Galactic Center (black hole, or membrane to the realm of Source and a doorway opening back and forth from Supreme Creation to Individual Creation). In fact, the Big Bang Theory of Einstein could be noted here. For passing through this membrane from the lower dimensions, we leave behind the power of Time, Space and Gravity and enter pure Existence. From Higher Dimensions to lower dimensions, pure light shapes to realities of consciousness that move through the membrane and collide with Higher Intent to Manifest. Pure Existence is on a collision course with Space, Time and Gravity (which is on a collision course with Pure Existence). When the collision occurs, a new world exists.

Are we presently on a collision course to exit the 4th World in order to enter the 5th World? So the Mayan, Hopi and other Shamans tell us. We are already noticing the time collision as it seems to disappear minute-by-minute.

For what purpose would we enter this dimension? To extract the higher intent of the New World and to know and understand the power of existence we can use as we enter this paradigm of a new existence.

Twelfth Dimension – Beyond Time, Space and certainly Gravity, the essence of Source is met in the 12th Dimension. No limit to light occurs. The experience of Nothing and the experience of Everything are known, but not definable. The aeon condition of the abyss is felt. This indefinite energy of consciousness is visited by the individual in order to gain from the Well of All Knowing the power and the mystery of life. This energy is absorbing and absorbed. Intuition is used to feel and decipher this energy field. You can gather this energy by command (intended focus: I desire this energy to bring the knowing of [your name]).

What good will it do? When a mystery illness occurs, the insights or messages of what can be known may be extracted. When a mystery of life (such as what is our next world going to be like) is to be explored, then the intention is set to gather the wisdom of the new world. It is good to know that you will not likely bring back an immediate answer. However, be willing to let the formulation of the insight string into the lower dimensions and formulate through symbols and shapes until configuration of a language can be used.

Thirteenth Dimension – I know as soon as I say this is the highest dimension we can reach, someone will prove there is more. So be it. However, as I trust the messages of the Divine, this is our present Nirvana. It is our last expanded state of consciousness that we can tap into until we are more prepared through our S.E.M.P.E.S., our Physical and Spiritual DNA and our intent to live in Union. We must live this before we move beyond it. When we live it, we will need the 100th Monkey to bring us beyond this Dimension. How will it look when we can pass it? It will look to us in this Earthly dimension that we can end the fight and struggles within ourselves and amongst ourselves. It will look like peace is prevailing and harmony is the rule not the exception. This 13th Dimension is Pure Love and No Thing is the experience of Light and No Limit to Light in this state of consciousness. We can journey to this point of existence to live in Peace, Love and Harmony. Again, absorption of Source occurs and merges with us as we merge with this ubiquitous substance/ no substance. It is important to not expect to bring a language forward, but simply a radiance that will continue to extend from our electromagnetic field and into consciousness in the lower dimensions.

This has been quite a journey through the Path of Living and the Triad of the Higher Self. Absorb this knowledge and you will be well on your way to manifesting your desires. Review this part of the book again, and again. Note how you are using the energy described and revealing how you are the Living Tree of Life. Take time to color any sphere or path on your Tree of Life form.

From the Higher-Self realm of consciousness, we descend the Tree and enter the Soul Realm where the natural qualities of Source are centered and released to the individuated state of being.

Part III

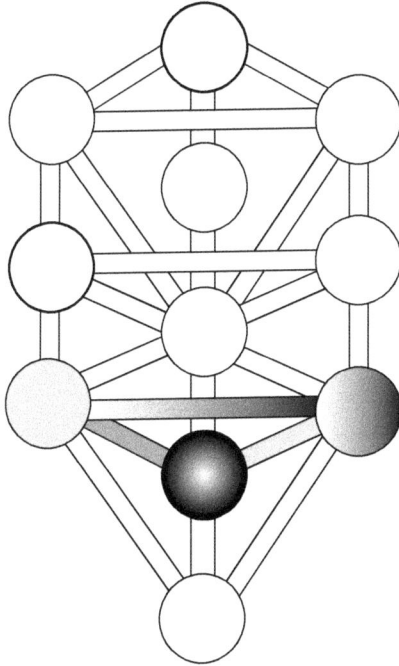

The Soul Triad

A MANIFEST STORY

Before continuing our journey climbing down the Living Tree, I want to share a Manifest Story with you. It began in the late 1980s during spiritual counseling sessions with a couple of young women. They had the desire to open a metaphysical bookstore. Their desire was intense, but the project was not getting off the ground. They prayed, meditated, affirmed and did everything dictated by the powerful authors who were experts on how to manifest. Still, nothing happened.

Then, they signed up for one of my classes to study the Tree of Life. As I indicated to them, and the students studying with them, if dedicated to the work being presented, they could follow the power of Source and manifest dreams and desires. I asked each person to feel deeply within and decipher what they *really, really, really* wanted. I sent them home for the week to meditate and enter their sacred place within. They were instructed to listen carefully and express what they wanted to manifest. A week later, these two women came back to ask, "Can we jointly work together and manifest the bookstore?" I affirmed they could and they diligently set out to accomplish this manifest by following the wisdom and conscious flow of the Tree of Life.

Week after week we met. The group flowed with the information and was so in tune with it, that when they arrived at class, they were already living through the next sphere of consciousness that we were to study. In fact, the two women were exposing experiences for setting the foundation and opening their store right along with the course of study. On the night we were to explore the Sphere of Splendor, they announced that they were going to sign a contract for space to set up their store with a building owner. I chuckled and revealed to them that the Sphere of Splendor held the power of setting into motion contracts and commitments for the future.

Our studies continued and as we entered the Sphere of Kingdom, the women announced they were ready to open the doors to the store and invited all of us to the Grand Opening Ceremony. Yes, what they *really, really, really* wanted occurred and their Spiritual Intent was fulfilled.

Soul Triad and Pathways

VEIL: DESTINY OF SOUL-TO-MATTER

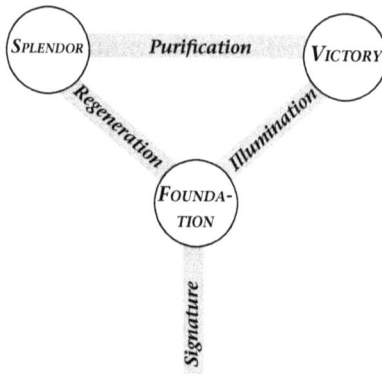

Another veil is rent. The place of consciousness in this Triad of the Universal Mind is very focused on the Soul, the individuated quality of Source. The foundation is set in this Triad for the Soul's evolution to prepare to explore matter. In this evolution of consciousness, more separation is felt. It can be called the *Evolution of Separation* and the state of the individual feeling lesser than the Creator. However, the Creator is the Separation – is the Soul – is the Experience. In the individuated quality, a personal self is emerging carrying an appearance of one of many and therefore, an illusion that separation exists.

The previous triad, the Higher-Self Triad, receives the gifts of the Monarchy imprinted into the Child of Source – the Soul. The Child, taking the position of monarchy in the Soul Triad, prepares to birth the realm in which it will reign, and imprints the intention in the Womb of the Soul. The central sphere of this triad is called Foundation and relates to the womb. This acknowledges that the foundation of all life is set while in the creative evolution of gestation occurrs in the womb-of-consciousness. In fact from the first triad, we note the Sphere of Understanding is the Womb of the Universe and the Great Mother releasing every soul into being. In the Soul Triad, the Womb of Humanity is recognized and releases each soul into a personal existence.

The Womb of the Soul Triad is a reflection of the Supernal Triad and the Higher-Self Triad. Simply an unfolding of consciousness is occurring. All that is released in the higher regions of consciousness is preparing to explore a particular realm that will best support the individual experience and a particular level of focus. It is here that the central point (Foundation) of this triad is the memory bank of humanity and has the storage of Soul Evolution (lifetime-after-lifetime), and is a storehouse for Divine knowledge that each soul connects with, gleans insight from and gathers strength while journeying through the Realm of Unknowns (Earth).

This triad is also referred to as the Astral Triad. The 'astral' is the substance that creative thoughts and emotions build upon Divine Intention and cause the development of matter to occur. The Astral Triad is also the state of our collective unconscious and personal unconscious. It is the archetypal energies used in dream time, meditation and visions to allow the energies of the Universe to be used and even formed into an experience. It is the storehouse of personal experiences and memories that we often dip into. Collectively, we develop our world via the webbing of personal beliefs. Personally, we develop our world through experiences in the Earth existence. The collective state of conscious is impacted by both personal experiences and spiritual alignment. It is an important place of consciousness to understand so we move out of the shadow and into the light.

In many spiritual languages, the astral plane of existence is seen as the illusionary plane. It is, and it is not. It carries great value and the illusion is simply our forgetfulness that we are a part of the Whole and the belief that building on our personal memories is all there is. We are not just our past or our memories. When we are caught in the web of past energy releasing intentions, we are in illusion of separation from Source Self that has no past, no present and no future. It simply IS. In exploration, the individual qualities break down the Whole to see the components and in that flow recognize a past, present and future as well as time, space and gravity; but ultimately recognize the Whole. Identification occurs in the cycling consciousness.

Let's look at a quasi-scientific reality of whole and parts. If a scientist has a human body to dissect, the first reality is that he has a whole being. When the body is broken down into parts, the scientist gets to see the components of the whole, identify the components, and yet, the whole exists – it is not separate. It is the concentration on the components of the whole that creates a separation as each tissue, bone, muscle, organ, etc. is placed into a focused review. As we see the components of Source, we are the scientist dissecting the whole in order to explore what it is, what it has and what is occurring. We are in a focused review as we explore life-after-life and uncover the components (animal, plant, mineral, human, intergalactic and more) of Source. The Soul Triad provides a more focused view of the parts.

The three spheres of swirling light in this Triad provide the following qualities of living:

+ Victory: The Eternal Victory
                 Deemed: Devotion to the Soul
                             Pattern

+ Splendor: The Perfect Outcome
                 Deemed: The objective of Source
                             to bring perfection into
                             manifestation

+ Foundation: Stability
                 Deemed: Evolutionary patterns
                             of the Universe

More definition occurs as the rays of light are released through the pathways extending from each sphere. As you note in the view of the Soul Triad, an energetic vibration releases the experience of purification as energy flows from Victory to Splendor. From Victory to Foundation, the power to illuminate the inner consciousness is released. Splendor puts forth the ray of light, which is the gift to regenerate the higher-self into the personal qualities. The signature, which is the imprint of Source, is brought into the world from the Sphere of Foundation and into the Sphere of Kingdom.

In this Triad, more personal expressions will be noted. The call to be more attentive with your desire to manifest what you *really, really, really* want is needed. It is in this Triad that the World of Formulation is quite strong. It is the place of consciousness that needs exceptional awareness or the challenge of distortion or abortion of a desire occurs. As each sphere and path is dissected to help your awareness remain keen, use the knowledge of creative imagination to carve the ideal of your desire and allow your mental and emotional self to set the foundation with congruency in thought and feeling. Your T.E.A. needs to be brewed to perfection. You are the Living Tree and this function of your tree requires awareness. Reviewing the next three spheres of consciousness will help you brew your T.E.A.

SPHERE 7 – VICTORY

Emerald green circles and twirls, stirred by the path of transformation from the Higher-Self Triad. The final sphere of the Pillar of Force is activated as Victory vibrates the intent of the Universe as noted and supplanted from the Spheres of Wisdom and Mercy. Personal creative force is released. To assist the use of this creative force, your heart is brought to your mind. This creates the instincts and emotions to be in joint tenancy with your intellect and the active energy of the Pillar of Force.

Fluid and ever-shifting shapes of the power of creative visualization occur. Flowing forward and backwards over the boundaries of manifestation, the formula and formulation takes shape in this state of consciousness. From the Supernal Consciousness to this sphere of consciousness, the brain of humanity develops with the imprint of All Knowledge woven into the minds of personal expression. In the state of soul consciousness and individual consciousness, your brain is forming "tracks" of information that you use to create realities out of your desires.

Ancestors and ancient philosophers noted from this sphere in the evolution of consciousness, that you will only create what you are capable of creating. That capability depends on your beliefs. If you are uncertain of your beliefs, revisit the path of Angelic Support from the previous Triad and glean an understanding how your beliefs influence the power to manifest your desires. Also, the Sphere of Mercy combined with the Sphere of Victory helps you expand your consciousness to create greater abilities that will influence your Soul-Mind.

The state of consciousness in Victory helps you move through the 'Peter Pan syndrome' of Illusion and Immaturity. This is the "I don't want to grow up" syndrome that keeps you from fully manifesting what you feel so passionately you want to see in your personal reality. Through this sphere, the Divine Mind influences the instinctive mind with love and refines the energy to assist the greater ability to create and connect with the Whole. As you move past the Peter Pan syndrome, you grow through love of the Divine, yourself and others. This absolutely helps you shape-shift your dreams and desires into a form that can manifest and not be lost in the illusion that can or will distort the outcome.

The Sphere of Victory is the last sphere of the Pillar of Force. It receives the energy of Mercy and transmits it to Splendor, Foundation and Kingdom. It carries the Power of Force and assists in changing polarities. Masculine moving to receptive Feminine occurs, which allows the inflow of Universal consciousness into the Personality. In fact, this sphere of consciousness is known as the first Sphere of the

Personality, which reflects your own, individual desires back to Source. Your desire is the vehicle of the soul to manifest and the principle of Source and to integrate it through the personality (and vice versa).

This sphere is the polarity of the Soul Triad in conjunction with Splendor. It carries the Occult or *Hidden* Intelligence. This is the very brilliant quality of the universal intellectual virtues, which are perceived by the viewpoint of the intellect and the contemplation of faith. It is the force of living the wisdom of Source through the many aspects of consciousness. It is termed, "hidden" because it is held within the unconscious and only found by the Seeker who seeks the hidden wisdom of the Creator. We cannot see even the lowest of frequencies of energy, but we know they are here to be used. We strive to understand that the Rays of Source radiate from above where all energies flow and are distributed to all existence. Devotion to the soul pattern occurs without conscious knowing until we connect and relate to the Soul through inner contemplation/inner communication (meditation) and connect with the Rays of Light Within.

Devotion to the Inner Path of awareness provides the Spiritual Experience of a vision of the Beauty and Triumph of the Creator. Inner balance initiates the Vision of Beauty and Victory and then resides in the activities of human life. The Vision of Beauty is the sight and feeling that all life is in harmony and order, while Victory is the experience that, "all" that has been desired "Is." Soul Will united with creative ideation and personal desire provides beauty in manifestation. Beauty is everything in synchronization.

As synchronization occurs, the virtue of this path is released into consciousness. This virtue is Unselfishness. Once you have unlocked the doorway of your Soul, you will discover that selfishness is no longer needed for you will have found what you have been searching for. This doorway is unlocked through educational systems of many levels (maturation). Self-Awareness comes through the pathways of education which include

+ Family and community experiences

+ Schools of childhood

+ Higher Education (College)

+ Self-Awareness

+ Spiritual Education

+ Higher Awareness - Applying what you learn

Love exists in Self-Awareness but to get to unconditional love, which is Unselfishness, you must develop personal awareness and self-acceptance. This comes by way of the unfolding path of maturity.

The vice of this sphere is Lust or Unchaste, Misused Sex. This is the result of a lack of self-acceptance and outer referencing (the need to find that others love us).

Lust is the over-emphasis or exaggeration of force:

+ Power

+ Material acquisitions (including people)

+ Knowledge (to believe I am intelligent)

+ Sensate Satisfaction (if I can touch it, it is mine)

Being unchaste simply means that you are not Pure of Heart. You hide within yourself, or close off your emotions out of fear of rejection, unworthiness or an inability to know yourself.

Misuse of sex is the Lower Ego needing to "feel" as though

one has control of their life (or others) and the compulsion to "Get what I want," regardless of consequences. A person forces sex onto another to manipulate outcomes. Of course, sexual force is also outright rape. Misused sex is a connection only with the sensate world with the hope of providing physical gratification, which serves only the lower world. The Higher order of sex is the connection with the sensate, the Union with Soul and the Union with Spirit (The Union with the Triads Above and Below).

Archangel Haniel holds the grace of this matrix and reveals the intent of Victory of the Universe. Three names are given to this angelic being with all representing different aspects of the same angel:

◆ **Archangel Haniel – Divine Grace**

- Brings forth the Truth of Beauty and Harmony and helps establish it in the lower world
- Provides Grace of the Divine and asks us to be capable of receiving it.
- Shows the way to take dominion over emotions
- Assists in balancing human sexuality
- Opens gate to Beauty so miracles can occur
- Opens gate to Foundation so birthing occurs
- Helps us feel our God/Goddess nature
- Aids teachers and leaders
- Wrestled with Jacob who changed his name to Israel (Mystically maimed his leg)
- Jacob means mental/animal consciousness of humanity

◆ **Archangel Auriel – Light of God**

- Receiving the force of the Sun (Son)
- Lamp to show the way
- Stirs the artist, writer, musician within
- Inspires joy

◆ **Archangel Phanael – Face of God**

- Manifestation of the Divine in All Things
- Balance that ensures proper force for the pattern of all
- Love, Joy, Ecstasy which comes from the meeting of inner and outer Divinity
- Indwelling Divine Principle joining with its counterpart in another human (true love/soul love); or recognizes this reflection in the beauty of art, the sunrise/sunset, a dance, flow of joyful life being seen in others.

The nature of consciousness in this sphere represents the desire, nature or motivation of the Divine Human to express its perfection. It is the living cells of Source creating Its reality through the desire nature motivating the collective humanity to create. This inspires your inner-self to know your Divine Self, which will always help you meet your needs.

This sphere is an energy of consciousness that encourages sacred and religious attitudes. These attitudes help us not to forget the Ultimate Source as we journey through the individual passageways of life that appear separate from The Creator.

When you are aligned in this level of existence, it moves you beyond the sensate world and encourages your connection and recognition of the vibrating Universe seen through all life. When you flow into the vibration, you are called to take dominion over the sensate world so you can take charge of the energetic outcomes that manifest through your desire nature. You refrain from the profane and celebrate through reverence of life, union with a higher order and the power to create oozes through your personal expressions. You become capable of aligning with specific vibrations and mastering them, such as:

+ Love, Fertility, Cultivation

+ Commerce, Transport and Transformation

+ Spiritual Goals and Arts

+ War and Peace

+ Agriculture

+ Protector of Youth, Law, Justice and the Weak

+ Time

+ Karma

+ Astronomy/Astrology

+ Transmutation

This is the Realm of Eternity or Repetition. It causes the repetition and sustaining power of the physical and psychological patterns of the atomic level of existence. It is an instinctive and involuntary process within your inner consciousness. It creates the circulation of facts contained within the unconscious mind and accepts them as a part of the memory bank – forming habits:

◆ On the creative level, the soul is nourished

◆ On the spiritual level, repetition facilitates union with one's own Divinity (the joy and ecstasy is indescribable when this occurs)

◆ It also is the repetition of life-after-life providing constant learning for the soul

◆ It can hold the negative power of repeating old and no longer usable attitudes, feelings and actions that need to be transmuted in order for you to grow to higher levels.

The ray of light radiating from this sphere provides the energy of motivation, activity and ceremony. The ceremonial process provides the alignment with the Higher Order and reflects Source in the realms of the individual. Personal and creative power is released. As long as you know what it is, you will use astral energy very well to develop the ideal of a dream or desire. Know what you are doing with your mind and heart so you create exactly what you want. Learn, feel, know the vibration of love which is the cohesive energy drawing all components into oneness.

The two paths that Victory ignite to assist the effervescent flow of the Soul Triad are Purification and Illumination. They form the conduits of important energy fields to help you set the foundation of your desire into perfect order.

PATH OF PURIFICATION

This pathway carries dynamic, interactive energies that support the Soul intent to manifest, while maintaining an awareness of the Source Consciousness that is expressed in all living matter.

The simple word, "purification," releases the wisdom of clearing out, providing holiness in the soul of the individual and helping the lower ego know of the higher intent from within. The root word, "Pure," reveals the knowing that all is an unadulterated expression of the Whole. Thus, the word, "purification" provides the wisdom that a constant removal of contaminants (lesser thoughts, unworthy attitudes and negative communication) is occurring all the time through the active power of this path of consciousness.

The red glow of light encourages the Exciting Intelligence or Active Intelligence. This intelligence is tumultuous, creating the chaos of creative thinking and the excitement that inspires transformation, which allows the creative forces to be utilized by your mind and emotion for manifesting purposes. It is an exciting thought that moves you to a passion to form activities and opportunities to manifest your desire. It is the stimulus to do something with your desire.

Key to this path of active intelligence is "mouth" – your mouth and the mouth of the Creator. Note that from the Logos (Word of Source) the Primal Vibration issued forth the Original God-Goddess Energy and Intent. And like a lightening bolt, It dashed everything into being. Matthew 4 verse 4 says, "...it is not by bread alone that man can live, but by every word which proceeds from the mouth of God."

There is an important message behind these words. It is a constant reminder that nothing manifests without the spoken word, and in truth, every word is from the mouth of the Creator. You only have bread because it is a spoken intent to have bread. You do not have anything until you can take the inspiration, think it, feel it, create with it, and allow it to unfold in the path of worldly development by speaking of it. Your words are the purification or the destruction. Your words are the final outcome calling the desire into manifestation or abortion.

Words spoken carry a positive or negative (double edged sword) and create and manifest from the power invested in them (strength of positive or strength of negative). Note the importance of listening to the words within to gathering the power of true energy. Speak words as though you are God/Goddess speaking and realize what you will manifest.

Exciting Intelligence is profound. It reveals the power that speech offers:

+ Manifested thought through the spoken word.

+ A vehicle for creative expression of the Principle of Life

+ An intense cosmic event occurring (Spirit and Matter becoming one)

+ Power of Utterance – Living and Expressing the Divine Word

Bring your words to a higher vibration by uttering purely:

+ Your Mastery

+ Your True Intent

+ Your Love of Life

+ Your desired outcomes

The Law of Purification is activated on this path, as well as in the Sphere of Severity. Its vibration provides the existence of experiencing, releasing and rebirthing. It is a constant reminder that the Universe Itself constantly releases cycles, clearing the old and purifying Its existence to allow the substance of life and the personal events of the soul to experience the Whole Unadulterated existence. Impurities

of structures, thought, word and feelings are released. Innocence (pure Source) is gained so a new cycle may occur without the existence of old influences. From Purification comes
Pure Existence.

In the Path of Purification, the act of purifying your language as well as your life experiences is very important. It is
important that you speak what you know is truth. Truthfully
speak what you want. Do not caveat your speech for the
sake of others' desires, feelings and perceptions you may have
about them. Above all, consciously choose to speak as the
Divine, holding the intent of a pure outcome.

Take time to uncover what your language produces most
of the time. It is so very important to know how you speak
about what you want at one moment. Discover if you automatically define it in another way, or abort it in the next moment by speaking of fears or old beliefs as to why you cannot
achieve your desire. Do you find yourself

+ Repeating cycles = holding on to the old influences?

+ Continuing to repeat words and phrases that hold
  your fears and rejections of Mastery?

+ Continually holding on to objects that you no longer
  use?

What are other ideas you have about repeated cycles that
hold you back from successful relationships, careers, creative
expression, health, abundance?

The Path of Purification joins the Spheres of Victory with
Splendor. These also reveal purification areas. Victory is the
purification of emotions/feelings. In Victory, the heart is
brought to the head on the Pillar of Force/Masculinity, where
the head can review and deduce (arrive at a fact via the power
of reasoning) any illusionary emotions.

In Splendor, the purification will be of the mind because the mind is brought to the Heart on the Pillar of Form/Feminine and will allow the mind to soften from its rigid rationalization (attempt to justify an action or attitude with logical reasoning) and intuit the Truth.

PATH OF ILLUMINATION

This path enamors me. It is my constant reminder of being connected with Source, even in the world of illusionary patterns of separation. It is a path that connects the desire nature of Sphere Seven, Victory, with the automatic nature of Sphere Nine, Foundation. It releases Natural Intelligence within the automatic consciousness of humanity. This intelligence provides the weaving of remembering how to live in Unity with the Divine Mind rather than floating in the Collective Conscious of the world and our subjective conscious or our subjective subconscious maladies.

Connected to the Universal Desire Nature, we can know the interchange of love. Unconsciously, we may believe we carry love. But if we cannot feel it, we will subjugate it according to our beliefs, judgments and fears. However aligned with this path, we connect with "The Secret Place of the Most High" and learn it within the brain of the Illumined Adept (very skilled or proficient individual who is using the intent of Higher Intelligence).

Natural Intelligence reveals the perfected nature of all that exists. It provides our individual knowing with the awareness that there is no distinction from natural and supernatural because everything is in its natural and pure state. Through the natural process of evolution, everything that seems supernatural comes into the state of being common. For instance, the box sitting in our living rooms that radiates talking pictures and educational information as well as entertainment shows was once considered strange and unnatural and seen as magic by primitive peoples. Now, the television is commonly used and understood by most people throughout the world. We most certainly can take this analogy further with iPods, iPhones, and technologies used in medicine, other sciences and games. This was all a science fiction story not too many decades ago. On this pathway, our Divine Heritage through the process of evolution provides a continual uncovering of the "secrets" of the Supernatural Realm. The Divine Mind holds and expresses everything that ever was or ever will be (television, computers, telephones, healing vibrations, mind expansion, etc.) and in this path we can uncover and enter into a land of understanding it all.

We live this Natural Intelligence all of the time. We become more clearly aware of it through:

✦ Understanding Universal Laws

✦ By living the Truth of Natural Intelligence (remembering that everything is natural)

✦ Opening our states of awareness to Natural Intelligence through Meditation

The root of the power of this path reveals that through meditation, we can understand the qualities of Nature. Through meditation, we learn how to be patient while we connect to the wisdom of this intelligence as we dip into the ocean of consciousness and search through the depths of our psyche to discover the Greater Truth. Meditation offers the power to flow through the vessel of consciousness that opens to the stream of the unbroken flow of knowledge. In the philosophy of the Tree of Life, you step into the flow of knowledge through meditation via symbols. This allows the knowing you will stumble on the wisdom and constellation of knowledge that is all around you in its most natural form. Symbols provide the way and means to hook into the Mind of the Divine and let intuition flow, providing the wisdom needed. Seek to understand symbols.

When you want to align with the perfect order of your desire, meditation is a key factor. It not only allows you to "talk with God," it helps you form the astral energies into right order and design for the final outcome. Often it has been said that what you desire is Creation asking you to bring to matter that which Creation has already designed. You are the final artist of the design and most certainly the instrument that will put the design to use in your personal reality. Meditate, find the design, finish sculpting it in your heart and mind, and prepare it for the realm of matter.

To further your design and help the energy flow into the realm of matter, the Law of Luminosity and Illumination comes into action in this pathway. This Law reveals that the non-living and living quality of everything possesses the ability to respond to higher degrees of Intelligence. An inward development and awakening provides the illumination of the Light of Intelligence that is within. It is encoded within your Soul to seek the Light and constantly urging feelings motivate you to take action to reveal the Light.

Luminosity provides the inner search to discover our inner Light, while Illumination provides the means to radiate the Light. We assist the process by clearing the inner consciousness of false beliefs, perceptions and fears. We increase the clearing through the vortices of Light called 'Chakra Centers.' As this process is repeated, we reveal levels of separation from the higher power within. Each Chakra Center holds vibrational energy with conscious intelligence. I take the liberty here to describe the thirteen Chakras and their association to dimensions within the universe and their Esoteric Colors (different than the standard rainbow description commonly used).

+ **_Root Chakra_** – Balances: Physical and financial security, physical health, family history, sexual, grounding to Earth matrix, past life karma. Serves to enhance existence and survival. Adrenals, spinal column, kidneys and fertility. **1st Dimension.** Indigo color.

+ **_Sacral Chakra_** – Balances: Creativity, soul purpose, feminine energy, female issues, healing of sexual/sensual conditions, financial blockages, Inner Child, loss and ongoing. Purification and cleansing. Throne of the Soul. Reproduction system. Fertility. **2nd Dimension.** Red color.

+ **_Solar Plexus Chakra_** – Balances: Self-esteem, expression in the world, masculine energy, ego, male issues. Balancing of the will. Establishing personal power, confidence and healthy boundaries. Stomach, liver, gall bladder and nervous system. **3rd Dimension.** Violet Color.

+ **_Heart Chakra_** – Balances: Giving and receiving love, love of self, dealing with sorrow, grief and honoring higher self. Compassion. Awakening and discovering the spiritual heart. Heart, thymus, blood and circulation. **3rd Dimension.** Yellow color.

✦ ***Throat Chakra*** – Balances: Communication, ears, nose and throat (hearing, discerning and speaking), speaking truth, expressing self, memory/past life. Creative self-expression. Encourages the personal witness. Ears, nose, throat, thyroid and lungs. **3rd Dimension.** Green color.

✦ ***Brow Chakra*** – Balances: Intelligence, balance of right/left brain, intuitive/psychic. Connection to the spiritual witness. Pituitary Gland (balance/imbalance). Third eye, right/left brain and nervous system. **3rd Dimension.** Blue color.

✦ ***Crown Chakra*** – Balances: Spirituality, Alignment with God/Goddess, Expanded Consciousness, Pineal Gland (balance/imbalance). **3rd Dimension.** Soft Yellow color.

TRANSPERSONAL CHAKRAS

✦ ***8th Chakra*** – Aligns you with the 4th Dimension, Sound of the Universe, interaction with Guardians. Harmonizing and coordinating the ethereal and emotional bodies. Immune system balancing. **4th Dimension.** Very light yellow color.

✦ ***9th Chakra*** – Connection to the rhythm of the Universe and the rhythm of all things: nature, galaxies, universal laws, etc. Coordinating and balancing the higher mental. **4th Dimension.** Aqua color.

✦ ***10th Chakra*** – Conscious blending with the Divine Mind. Inspiration and aspiration enhanced. Harmonizing and coordinating the mental body to the astral body. **5th Dimension.** Pearl Gold color.

✦ ***11th Chakra*** – Connecting with the Womb of the Great Mother. Purpose of Higher Manifestation. Harmonizing and integrating the astral with the causal body. **6th Dimension.** Crimson color.

✦ ***12th Chakra*** – Connecting with the God-Head. Power of Being. Blessing of Higher Consciousness. Pure Potential. Harmonizing and integrating the causal body with the spiritual body. **7th Dimension and 8th Dimension.** Ultra Blue-Violet color.

✦ ***13th Chakra*** – Oneness. Beyond Awareness. No Thing/Everything. Purest Light. Harmonizing the casual/spiritual body with the Monad. Love, compassion and Devotion are enhanced. **9th through 13th Dimension.** Brilliant Light flecked with Gold.

ILLUSTRATION 9: 13 ESOTERIC CHAKRA CENTERS

As the Law of Luminosity and Illumination comes into the Realm of Matter, it is well to remember that we are able to recognize the Light of God/Goddess is within. We only have to awaken this reality by inner noticing the light frequencies we carry through our Chakra Centers. As we are aware, we release the Light into the world of our present existence. This enhances our personal experiences and brings them to harmonious realities.

Victory has taken place in the evolution of the soul. Now the flow of excitement of the Creator can be seen in the next sphere.

SPHERE 8 – SPLENDOR

The blinking light of orange radiates an active attraction as you prepare to gather the wisdom of the Sphere called Splendor. In fact, the Spiritual Experience of this path is the *Vision of Splendor.* It is the realization of the Glory of the Divine Father/Divine Mother manifesting in the Created World of Matter. It is called the Joy of God celebrating the Creation of Expression in individual matrices, designs and forms. It calls you to remember:

✦ Behind all created things is the Creator

✦ Nature is the Garment of the Creator

✦ You are nature

✦ Everyone is the Co-Worker/Co-Executive of the Creator.

This sphere holds the energy of the Covenant – The agreement between the Soul-Self and Creator-Self to manifest and live in the realm of matter. The Covenant activates the Spiritual experience. Your Spiritual Experience is the Vision of Splendor as you recognize that you truly are a co-executive and artificer (one skilled in making things). You become the Alchemist through the realization that you are Manifesting within the Created World. Your very act of creating is the Union with Higher Consciousness and the dominion you have over the world of matter. You bring order to disorder, manifest from the ethers (astral) and create the equilibrium of the two worlds (non-matter and matter).

The Power of Sound from the path of Purification instigates energy in the Sphere. It stirs the defining moment of that which is to manifest by naming it. By naming intentions the potency for manifestation occurs. The voice, filled with energetic congruency of mind, emotions and spirit creates the vibration of the matrix and the structure of the personal reality of the desire. Invocations, such as prayer, chants, and affirmations help to clarify, define and bring into matter, the ideal of the desire. The Covenant comes alive in life by these acts.

This sphere initiates the virtue of Truthfulness and Honesty. For only through these qualities can you absolutely manifest your desires. Truth and honesty call forth the exacting of the vibration and not the distortion of the vibration. If the virtue is not in use, then likely the vice of this path is the wavering energy influencing a distorted outcome. The vice is Falsehood, Dishonesty and Criticism (of self and others). It keeps you from the power that belongs to you. It disables the full extent of the outcome of your desires.

To help you maintain the integrity of this state of consciousness and to hold the matrix of this state of Universal Consciousness, Archangel Raphael is the active principle angelic help. Raphael helps you decipher the contract of the intention and maintain clarity of mind and matter. Raphael helps you know when things are going too far (thoughts or feelings) that will create an imbalance. As an Angel of Healing, Raphael will bring healing to the mind as well as the body. He will help you open the levels of communication with Source that will guide you on the path of your Divine Plan.

Archangel Raphael will send you subtle energetic impulses to help you learn from mistakes. (Wise people gain their wisdom by their mistakes; only the unwise deny their mistakes.) He will help you shift your consciousness. Known as the Angel of Prayer, Love, Joy, Light and Healing; Raphael will help you discover all of these qualities in your personal reality. Archangel Raphael inspires you to be social so you may learn from others and share your knowledge with others. He inspires you to be whole, complete, filled with peace and living with integrity so you may fulfill your Covenant to live the soul-expression of Source. He most certainly will help you think, speak and align with what you really want, by keeping you aware of your inner thoughts and emotions as well as the vision of your desire.

This Sphere of awareness, Splendor, mixes active and passive energy for potent, successful manifesting fields of consciousness. It is a field of awareness that helps you find the power of the Divine Mind within you. It helps you understand that obstacles on your path are opportunities to learn, mature and test your ability to discover the Higher Mind. It encourages adaptation through strife as you flex your skills via the power to move your mind.

Splendor is the Sphere of futuristic processing. It is the Knowing that your Vision is the Outcome. It calls you to think and project, speak, be and live as you desire to experience. It is the use of Personal Intellect that creates the final outcome. It reveals that your truth becomes the pattern from which you create your existence.

As you contemplate this sphere and take in the message of the Contract being set, it is a good time to write your own contract with Source around what you *really, really, really* want to manifest. Be willing to use all of the knowledge of the Spheres and Pathways you have already learned and know how you want to maintain the clear focus for what you want to manifest. As you do, you activate the next pathway, Regeneration, as it takes your higher desire into the Womb of Foundation and supports your manifestation.

Divine Letter Contract
Between Source and

_____

It is my desire to commit to the following contract with Source to assist in bringing to fruition the Power of Mastery in the Earth Realm. I am willing and ready to Serve the Divine through my own right actions and to assist humanity by living these actions. My commitment covers the following areas of life:

_____
_____
_____
_____
_____
_____
_____
_____
_____
_____
_____
_____

Signed: _____

On this Date _____, 20__

ILLUSTRATION 10:   DIVINE LETTER CONTRACT

PATH OF REGENERATION

As you enter this path, you are working with your Personal Identity. However, it is the path that initiated in the Sphere of Beauty and reveals your Soul is ready to express its Higher-Self into the World of Matter. In fact, this path helps you open to your Higher-Self through the Soul Triad. It confirms that you truly never can forget you are the Avatar, the Alchemist, the Master, and the Child who has inherited the World. This path is a reminder to be attentive, alert and aware of whom you truly are; for in so doing, you draw into matter all that is necessary to maintain balance, and bring forth manifestations that are needed, wanted and ready to exist.

To continue the assistance within each individual, Source implanted the Collective Intelligence within this path. Collective Intelligence is the synthesis and adaptation of all forms of universal consciousness administering the Laws that governs reality. Collective Intelligence is used by you through regeneration of your higher intelligence, right use of reason and the power of discernment that helps you deduce the celestial information that reveals the perfection of Source in all existence.

This path excites the frontal part of your head and is known as the Countenance. It provides awareness and clarity and is spiritually known as the place where the controlling element of the Higher Mind is concentrated. This path teaches that our human consciousness is the form through which the Life-Power is perfected and physically present. (Our ability to stay focused, alert and aware allows us to use this perfected energy).

Alchemy is a mysterious or paradoxical process and is an art of transmutation. Ancient lore talks of turning lead to gold (dross to higher power). To assist in the alchemy, or ability to change the dross wisdom to the higher alignment, the Collective Intelligence brings forth the power to "assemble, bring together, combine, unify, synthesize, and embody." Our reasoning mind has the power to collect data, information, guidance and direction. Through our reasoning power, we can characterize, understand and realize the potential of the information of the Universe for right use to create a manifest our desired reality or regenerate and create new realities. To take charge, we must understand that material forces of nature (Fire, Water, Air, and Earth) really are modes of conscious energy and we have charge over these elements via inspiration, emotional balance, mental acuity, and our physical ability to manifest. To do this, we must also understand that our Will Power needs to be directed by the consciousness of Source in order to form the right use of Collective Intelligence.

This path provides the best way to direct our will power through the Law of Regeneration. This Law expresses the truth that everything within the galaxies of life is the everlasting expression of Divine Perfection. From the most miniscule to the largest construct, each expression births, develops awareness at the level of its own species and allows for its decay and regeneration into the next field and evolution of Source. It begins again with rebirth in another, more advanced construct, with growth in consciousness. This is a constant cycling process of betterment that one can detain, but cannot stop. Detainment comes through Free Will and Choice. You have free will and choice to change your life right now. In the area you desire to master and create what you really want.

What choices are you making to do just that? This path will assist you in regenerating Right Choice for your perfect outcome.

SPHERE 9 – FOUNDATION

From the Path of Regeneration and the Path of Illumination, the Sphere of Foundation receives the vibrations of everything that is Above and places it into the developing womb of the human realities. Sphere 9, Foundation, is the womb. It is the development of every living cell of matter. It is the Omnipotent recognized in every cell of living consciousness. The cyclic and evolutionary pattern of the universe and the life-light that empowers the process is released into the soul of individuation in this sphere of consciousness. The provisions of consciousness used by each soul has virtually, unlimited authority or influence of the life experiences by the imprint of Source activated in the Sphere called Foundation.

The Empowerment of the Divine, alive within each Soul, brings about the Light of the Higher Self which is brought into existence through the unconscious Will of the Soul. This Will provides the ability to respond to the Will of the Divine through choice and resourcefulness of the Soul-Will. In order to experience it yourself, you must allow the Light to live through you by conscious intent.

You cannot isolate yourself in Spiritual Awareness, you must express that awareness through your existence and become a caretaker of the Earth and enhance your ability to manifest Spirit into Matter. This sphere of consciousness holds the victorious wisdom of such abilities.

Held within your personal psyche is the vision of the working of the Universe. The knowing how everything exists and weaves in the mind and heart of Source. This knowledge is obtained by clearing the unconscious of delusions, illusions and the pain and suffering from dysfunctional living. It requires the ability to live the Will of Truth (not your truth, not my truth, but the Truth of the Universe that is found in your subconscious memory bank).

This whole Triad calls you to the unconscious realms where you can release sacred knowledge. In so doing, you shape the cells of existence and the matrix of the form of your desires. You will need the gift of Higher Truth, gained by the right use of Discernment that awakens your ability to diagnose and determine what you need to change or enhance to bring your desire into the manifest world.

In this plane of consciousness, you learn to walk through the astral planes and into the higher planes of Wisdom and Truth, allowing you to discontinue the repetition of cycles of challenge and separation. In this state of existence, you learn the virtue of independence and individualism that allows you the freedom of taking charge of yourself rather than being controlled by others or the dysfunctional perceptions of your own unconscious. As you become independent and no longer controlled by others, your fears or false perceptions, you enter into individualism, which is the love of self and living from your Higher-Self. You detach from the lower world or lower states of survival and live with the knowing that you are able to master your personal reality as you live from your higher expression of Source materialized in a body.

If you find you cannot detach from co-dependency and the need to fulfill your dreams by others approval, you fall into the vice of Idleness, the state of not moving appropriately in the direction of your soul purpose. You will experience the non-productive use of energy, which is the expenditure of energy that produces worry, fear, fret and lack. You will feel as though you are moving against the current of life instead of going with the flow.

By the blessings of Source, when you feel you are in the struggle, the consciousness of the Archangel Gabriel is forthcoming. This is an Angel of Destiny and one who will help you regenerate your destiny, if you will choose to align with him. Gabriel will guide you while you journey through this state of consciousness on the universal Tree of Life.

Archangel Gabriel is given a title of the Angel of Destiny for the good works of speaking to Mary as he announced to her:

+ The pregnancy and birth of Jesus
+ The Resurrection of Jesus

It is also noted that he spoke to:

+ Mohammed and dictated the Koran to him
+ Joan of Arc and helped her assist the King of France

The Power behind these visitations brings awareness of the ability to speak and listen to the direction of the Divine to reproduce and rebirth, and to be directed to resurrect your Higher-Self. When listening to Archangel Gabriel, you may also hear the destiny of your desire that you are formulating as you travel the spheres and pathways of the Living Tree of Life. Are you listening? What do you hear?

Cycles and phases can be understood and worked within this place of consciousness. This wisdom provides vital understanding of how your dreams move from a desire, to a vision, to a manifestation and purpose. It is a place of Consciousness teaching you how to develop an ebb and flow of intentions, not a rush to get to the ideal, but the ability to allow the ideal to grow into a true substance of creation and usability in your life experiences. It teaches how to take action, when to relax and wait, and when to cultivate, perfect and manifest for use the desires you want to fulfill.

While you are in the incubation state of what you want to manifest through the Sphere of Foundation, remember your will and intent are important. You can clarify your will and intent through meditation and illuminating your Holy Inner Light. Regenerate the Light of Source within you, which stimulates unconditional love and the higher aspects of your true self. Let the cells of your ideal generate and expand while you help prepare the way for birthing you desires by clearing out any level of mind and emotion that are not congruent with your intent. Allow your automatic system to become the Higher Light of Source preparing the birth of what is important to manifest through you.

Be patient, for the imprint of your intent will be the signature you place on the outcome.

PATH OF SIGNATURE

In the philosophy of the Tree of Life, the signature is symbolized by an 'X' or a cross. It indicates the Signature of the Divine is imprinted on All. The 'X' or cross is a symbol of the union of the active and passive fields of energy coming together. It is the male and the female union. It is the Divine Father and Divine Mother as one and setting forth the Signature of Perfection into the Manifest world. The Signature means, "It is complete. It is finalized." It is the Omega. It is the Tao. It is the Most Dense energy. This vibration is called the Palace of Holiness and is the center from which everything else proceeds. As consciousness moves through this pathway, it honors that Which is Above is that Which is Below. It provides the awareness that the dream is fulfilled and ready to be utilized. We will understand more in the discussion of the Vehicular Triad, but for now, a review of this final path of the Soul Triad is of great importance.

As you enter this pathway, you are entering the Path of Self-Mastery. Your own imprint is placed on the world and your ability to administer your talents is released. Throughout this book you have been asked to know what you *really, really, really* want. This Pathway is the open door to the Manifestation. It is the open cervix of the womb of consciousness ready to birth your reality. It most certainly was the path of consciousness your soul traveled to birth into this human form you now reveal as the expression of Source in Matter.

You are embarking on the Path of Responsibility that asks you to take charge of your manifest. Soon, you will see if you have created your outcome. You will see if there are any distortions or did you abort your manifest along the way? If you have been sure of what you really wanted, and realized what you have asked for, then you have named it and are ready to claim it. When you name, you commit to be the caregiver of the birth, growth and maturity of your manifest. In fact, you have created a vow and set the seal to anchor the idea into the realm of matter. You are prepared to use the intelligence of this path which is called, Administrative Intelligence.

Administrative Intelligence directs the performance of the Intelligence of All Living Things. It is the point of Boundless Light that permeates everything and is everything permeating Itself into a crystallization that forms and activates matter. The Light encompasses the letter 'X,' which is recognized as the Signature of the Divine. It is also known as the holy directions: East, South, West, North, Above, Below and Within. Each direction holds a sacred awareness within the realm of matter:

+ *East* – The power to breathe, use vision and see an outcome. The power to communicate and connect with the Unseen Masters.

+ *South* – The power to interact, grow, and live one's purpose. The power to live with passion.

+ *West* – The power to go with the flow, explore life's blessings and share wisdom. The power to create.

+ *North* – The power to manifest, know you are one of many and many of The One. The power to live in Faith.

+ *Above* – The power to recognize Source as the Spirit alive within you. The power to live unconditional love.

+ *Below* – The power to honor the individuation of Source through the essence of your Soul. The Power to desire.

+ *Within* – The recognition of your Inner Self, your Angelic Being, as the Center Point of Wholeness. The Power to Be.

To know this Path is to live the Law of Universality and the Law of Correspondence. You Live the Tree rather than wonder what the Tree of Life is. You recognize It within everything. The Signature Path directs and associates everything in the Universe. The Law of Universality and Correspondence reveals:

+ The branch of the Tree has all the characteristics of the Tree as a Whole, even when severed. (Review the story at the beginning of the book to remember your DNA is the DNA of Source).

+ Each person is a component of Source and is endowed with all the attributes of Source and can perform the same as Source.

+ All things are connected to all other things.

+ All Principles of the Universe and All Laws of the Universe are in existence and fully activated.

+ The Laws exude a vibration that offers a Gateway into the Divine Universal Mind.

As you connect with this path of consciousness, you connect with The Completion of the Great Work. Everything Beneath it (the manifest world) is complete and whole and the reflection of the Great Work.

Part IV

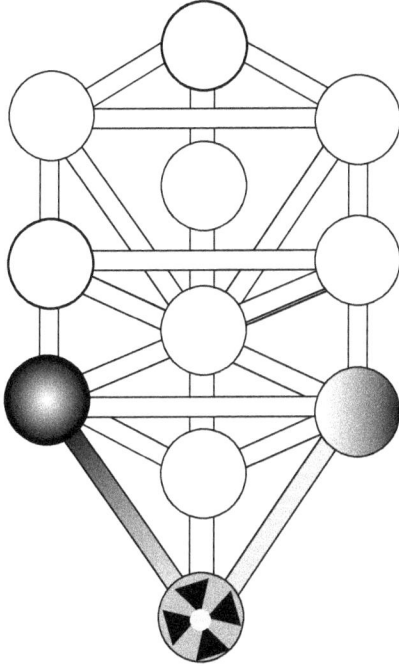

The Vehicular Triad

Vehicular Triad and Pathways

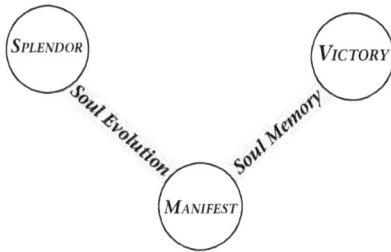

SPLENDOR

VICTORY

Soul Evolution

Soul Memory

MANIFEST

The signature has been placed. You have activated your power to manifest what you *really, really, really* want. In the philosophy of the Tree of Life, entering the Vehicular Triad indicates the Divine Manifest is set and the desire of Higher Consciousness is ready. Is your personal desire ready? Has it grown in the Womb of Consciousness? Are the contractions starting? Is the Vehicle ready to support the outcome?

The Creator's Vehicle is Earth, the people who inhabit the Earth and its animals, plants, minerals, fire, water and air. The Manifest Sphere is the final resting place of the journey from Above to Its expression Below. It is here that the complete manifestations of the energies of all the spheres of consciousness merge.

The Manifest sphere is the mirror of God/Goddess seeing Itself as human and human seeing itself as God/Goddess. The magic of this place of consciousness is the Divine Living Its Art form – Individuality. The magic for every human is the realization that manifesting occurs through urges of Source. It is evidenced as inspiration stirring independent thoughts, and emotional urges that stir personal action and formulation of the things you want to experience in your life. This realm is where you see individual dreams come to fruition. Earth is your vehicle to release actions, opportunities and full manifestation of your desires. It is your throne and place where you have dominion over the occurrences of life.

In this realm, the ability to see the different qualities of Source occurs. Ideas or ethereal dreams are no longer the major quality of consciousness. The material realities are structured and formed. The Tree reveals its unique roots, gnarling trunk, strong branches, unique leaves, beautiful flowers and nutritious fruits. The Paradise of Source unfolds and is discovered by those who strive to understand and recognize the sacredness of her soul and the beauty of Divine Expression beyond the veil of illusion.

The Kingdom of the individual is born and brought to bear in this sphere – the positive result of Source's Intention here existing in matter. "Thy Kingdom come, Thy Will be done, on Earth as it is in Heaven," is a statement solidifying the Great Work of Source recognized in this triad of consciousness through the Will to Complete. Each person needs this Will to Complete in order to manifest their desires.

The Vehicular Triad consists of the Spheres – Victory and Splendor as the duality and the Sphere called Kingdom, as the Center Point. It extends the energy of the Soul Triad, particularly the Sphere of Foundation into the Valley of Matter, birthing the Divine into physical form. This Triad also points downward, directing the influence of Source brought into Matter as the final manifest. The Liquid Light of Source pours into the grail cup of matter. The Soul is contained and the energetic influence of Earth is ready to be experienced. That which Is Above Is Below. The Unseen is seen.

The energetic influence at this point is earthly, solid, recognized and experienced. It provides the outer expression of Source. It connects Intuition and Intelligence with the active projection of form. In this realm, consciousness is brought to awareness in the 3rd Dimension, while all other dimensions move in unseen realities. Evolution of Separation is complete and Evolution of Union begins. The Return to Above is the quest each soul honors while exploring the individual components of Source in the Earthly sphere.

In addition to the Signature Pathway, two other pathways contribute to the final Sphere of Manifestation. They bring an influence supporting the consciousness of the individual and holding the power to remember the process and intent of the Higher Consciousness. The pathways provide the energetic influence of the Spheres of Victory and Splendor, bringing them into their final point for conscious use. They are not left in the fluidic or ethereal consciousness of life, but brought into the solid matter of existence. The individual is fully contained in the harmony of heart and mind combined to carry on the ability to express victory and the splendor of Being.

PATH OF MEMORY

This pathway, radiating a ray of magenta light, connects the Sphere of Victory to the Manifest Sphere. It brings the balance of emotion into the realm of matter. Contained within this path are great mysteries and sacred attitudes. This path reveals who you are, where you have come from, how you create living matter and your Return to your Sacred Oneness. It is your memory path that helps you recall that you are One as Source manifested in a human reality.

The enquirer is required to move deeply through the stratosphere of conscious and unconscious levels to discover the mysteries. Learning to travel the states of consciousness,

personal awareness, subconscious and universal consciousness provides the way. Training your mind to awaken into
the last two stages requires meditation and the art of altering
awareness through dimensional experiences. This wisdom-
path contained within The Living Tree brings forth another
reminder of the importance of meditation.

This path helps stir the memory of where you have
come from and how you will return, and it helps you remember who you are. You must learn to get beyond your
worldly and personal subconscious levels to comprehend
this mystery. This path assists you in doing so. It may take
you through passageways of old memories, perhaps through
strong dreams states, or previous life experiences, but it carries the intent to help you through the illusionary beliefs
that keep you stuck and separate. Through dedication, your
conscious and unconscious will break through the barriers
of limited memory and enter the realm of Universal Memory (connecting with all that Is, Was and ever shall Be). You
will connect with the Corporeal Intelligence of your personal self and Universal Self.

Corporeal Intelligence is cellular memory and allows you
to realize that every cell in your body contains the memory
of Source and Its intention to manifest in the world of Matter.
This path of awareness, through Corporeal Intelligence, calls
you to remember and understand many states of existence.
This intelligence of the Universe forms every structure of matter – galaxies, stars, and planets, physical bodies of mineral,
plant, animal and human. It initiates the growth of all bodies
(everything manifest and yet to manifest). It is the form of
intelligence within you that remembers exactly the original
matrix and structure of your soul desires. It already knows the
shape, dimension and foundation of what you *really, really, re-*

ally want to manifest. Flowing within this state of consciousness will help you remember the perfect matrix of what you want and most certainly will help you manifest it.

Forming your physical body, this path creates the Holy Living Temple of Source and the point of manifesting all desires. Your physicality is the container of Spirit in Matter. You hold it sacred by caring for your body and keeping it a clear temple for higher vibrations of existence. The Intent of Source is to use your personal unconsciousness to integrate wisdom through the millions of cells of your physical organism (memory cells). On this path, the part of your brain, the *medulla oblongata,* is where the specific structure, chemistry and function of Source releases memories through the human organism. The *medulla oblongata* is the connecting link between the higher brain centers, the spinal cord and the subordinate centers of the lower body. It governs respiration, heart rate, circulation, breathing and overall health-maintenance of your body whether you are awake or sleeping. It automatically keeps you functioning as Source embodied.

An Adept learns, through conscious discipline, to by-pass the involuntary quality of the *medulla oblongata* and demonstrates voluntary control over mind and body. He becomes a Master (Creator/Host) of the Vital Soul expressing in matter. To become the Master of the Vital Soul creates the ability to live consciously with soul-intent and higher purpose. Meditation and alignment with Higher Consciousness provides this ability, which allows one to build the "body" and "worlds" of consciousness through higher vibrations and live at higher dimensions, becoming One with the True Self.

One must learn to overcome the greedy, uncontrollable physical needs that seem to take control in the Manifest world. One must learn to take charge of the unconscious demands (emotional need-driven desires versus soul desires for higher evolution). One must learn to refine consciousness and seek to understand the Vital Soul and its evolution of consciousness through different lives, different experiences and different stages of growth. Then, the development, maturation and ripening of the soul to accept its Divinity occurs. You know what you truly want and you manifest it without distortion because you are the magician – aligned in the Oneness and able to transform ethereal energy into matter.

In Oneness is the reality of the ever-changing vibrations of Creation. The power of the Law of Life, Death and Rebirth is established on this path that allows for the power of changing realities to manifest, release and allow the next phase of existence to be experienced. Through this Law, we learn that everything is birthed from the Indestructible Divine Creator. We also learn that everything that is birthed, functions through its spiritual and chemical evolution and is released through its dying and transformation process, only to begin again. The continuum of life reveals a rebirth, yet, through the power of transmutation the new birth is a total change in form, is the nature of its new phase, or the substance of its new existence. Yet, it exists the same at its Spiritual Core – the Indestructible Divine Creator.

The energy to live, die and rebirth is contained within your cellular memory as two functioning chemical processes – on-going life and on-going death. There is no neutral chemical process within the body; everything is in a constant motion of living, dying and living again. When you learn the sacred mystery of this reality, you will also be able to display it in things you manifest. You will no longer have a need to possess items, people or opportunities. You will experience each in their right timing and dynamic qualities of the whole. You will release it all and turn the page of life to uncover the next process that is birthing, live it for a while, and release it into the ethers of wisdom for its next cycle of life, death and rebirth.

This wisdom allows you to flow with life, enjoy your manifests, release them when you are complete with them and create new realities again and again. It releases you from possessive or obsessive needs, for in truth you flow with the patterns of change and carry no worries for you realize all exists, transforms and exists in new realities.

The Path of Memory helps you remember the Sacred and Essential quality that you are. In doing so, you remember your Source Self and bring this awareness into your daily living in the Sphere of Manifestation. You transform with it through cycles and changes of life and you rebirth many times through the life events you experience.

PATH OF SOUL EVOLUTION

Exuding its crimson light from the Sphere of Splendor, the Path of Soul Evolution is a vital flow of energy necessary to activate the Vehicular Triad. This Path connects the Sphere of Splendor with the Sphere of Manifest reality. It brings the Mind of Reason into the intelligence of the Body. It weaves and anchors the covenant of the Soul, releasing life purpose of the soul journey into the activities of the physical reality. Here the Soul evolves through the stages of an Earthly life and leaves an imprint of wisdom of the journey for other souls to use as well. It certainly can be seen as a "Light on the Path."

The Path of Soul Evolution provides the fire of inspiration

– the drive and desire to empower, the wisdom to live in truth and integrity and the knowledge of how to fulfill soul-goals. Through each cycle of ever-evolving experience, the soul experiences aspects of Wholeness. The Soul-consciousness provides the urges from within to seek more knowledge and absorb the wisdom being learned by the Earthly experiences. It carries the vibration of Perpetual Intelligence and the ability to purposefully maintain awareness that is encoded from the consciousness of Source.

The power within this intelligence helps us maintain the ability to process and continually monitor our thinking, our assessments of experiences, our discernment of what is going on in our lives and what needs to continue or what needs to be released. It helps us become totally conscious of our inner process (the subconscious at work automatically, either directed by conscious intent or directed by unconscious resolutions – usually fears from past based realities filled with false perceptions or illusions).

Functioning in this state of consciousness provides the ability to use the eternal intelligence of Source and the fires of purification that burn away dross experiences from the past and create the evolution of awareness in the now. Accepting change provides the ability to stretch, extend or unfold consciousness beyond the limitation of false beliefs. This process empowers. Once empowered, the way is cleared to manifest true desires of the Soul.

Perpetual Intelligence provides the Soul with the never ending, never changing intelligence of Source. It is imprinted into the Soul and evolves through the manifest form of the human experience. Thus, the Law of Soul Evolution is activated on this path and is fulfilled in every human. This Law explains that every Soul is guided by the Divine Principle of Evolution.

Imprinted within each Soul is the drive and desire to grow and evolve, move into the Evolution of Union and reveal the true nature of living, which is Perfection – Source Itself.

The philosophy of the Living Tree of Life teaches the power of reincarnation is the ebb and flow of Soul Evolution. It is believed that each incarnation allows for experiences of wholeness, separation, polarities and the return to Oneness. As the physical world is so dense, not all experiences of the Divine state of consciousness can be taken in through one lifetime. The individuated aspects must be explored and experienced in order to reconnect, adhere to and blend with Wholeness as Perfection. In the blend, the Soul remembers its Source Self. To successfully accomplish this journey, the Soul must travel the pathways of time, space and separateness. Then learn to expand beyond time, understand and move beyond spatial realities, and overcome the belief in self versus Self. Perpetual Intelligence helps the Soul remember its wholeness while experiencing the individual parts.

While blended in consciousness with this path, the revelation of previous life experiences can occur. The right use of this knowledge is to integrate it, know what you have learned, use what you have learned and discontinue living the past life in the present incarnation. Each soul is called to integrate the knowledge and become one in the moment.

Finally, these two paths plus the Signature Path form a union with the Manifest Sphere and Completion of the Great Work occurs. Soul is embodied. Spirit is Matter. God/Goddess is expressed through individual forms.

SPHERE OF KINGDOM

The Kingdom is cultivated and prepared to receive the Master. The dominion of the monarch is activated in the Land of Matter. God and Goddess manifest and live as you and I, as plant and animal, as the whole nature of the Earth, the sky and the planets. The Divine Desire is manifest and each individual takes the position as monarch of their own existence. The Law of Completion is active and realized in this final vortex of light within the Living Tree.

This Law causes all manifestations to come into fruitfulness. The art of Source is complete and the individual Soul continues to use the power of Source Consciousness to execute and accomplish cycles and phases of evolution. Each individual continues to use this Law to complete ideas and desires. The plane of consciousness, called Earth, provides the means of completing all the principles of the Divine through right action and forming a manifest.

One principle that is most important to observe and act upon is that humanity must accept its Kingdom and take dominion. This can be done by learning the basic Esoteric Levels of Earth. It provides:

- ✦ The Celestial levels – to remain connected to the Divine
- ✦ The Astral levels – to set vibration of creation
- ✦ The Emotional qualities – to create
- ✦ The Mental capabilities – to formulate
- ✦ A Physical Vehicle – Temple to receive energy

This is the point of existence where you activate your dominion and allow your desires to manifest. It is where the results of your internal drive and desire to achieve what you *really, really, really* want, is brought to bear. This is the moment that the vital living power of Source within you is seen, felt and celebrated as the fruitful manifest of your creative imagination.

In this 10th Sphere of Light, multiple colors radiate revealing citrine, olive, black and russet. These colors represent the power to express in multitudes of differences. The manifest of every sphere and path of consciousness is contained and reflected through the structure of this sphere. Conscious, active, visible use of universal energies is known and experienced in this realm. This is the 'Below Living the Above.' For Humanity, this is the individual Soul living in matter, the personal self in the place of authority where Dominion of the world, nature, and one's own self occurs. Does humanity display this?

We still reveal an immature nature of our consciousness, yet evolving beyond the young adult. We truly are no longer the infant or small child. We are evolving states of consciousness recognizing our Source Self and our Empowered states of Being. As an individual, we recognize our mature qualities when we find life flowing more with grace, ease and the ability to overcome challenges by working through them. We notice maturity as we cultivate ways to maintain our awareness and union with Mother Nature and the whole nature of Life Itself. We display this awareness of our Dominion when we find ways to live in harmony with our brothers and sisters of humanity and when we grasp our Sovereignty and maintain it.

Ultimately, this plane of existence is guided by the spiritual reign or authority of the Divine Essence. Its *Resplendent Intelligence* illuminates the light of the Soul and shines it back to Itself. The Light and Life of Spirit is alive in form and the light and life of matter reflects back the vitality of Spirit through individual qualities manifested in the active field of conscious matter.

Here the Active and Passive poles form a union. The Sphere called Crown is the active Masculine force, and the Sphere called Manifest is the receptive Feminine form (thus called Earth Mother). Together, they shape the paradox of the unit of neither and both, and the quality of equality is experienced. Feminine energy governs the world of manifestation or form. Masculine energy enlivens it. One without the other does not fulfill the manifest – union and blending does.

The Kingdom brings into existence all of the essences represented by the nine other spheres of consciousness. As these aspects of Source are brought into manifestation, they create Light. This Light contains the Will of Source. The glory of the Light is the virtues and understanding brought forth through each sphere of consciousness. While the life of each Sphere depends on the original Sphere, Crown, their existence depends on the Kingdom Sphere. The universe could not have been created without the Sphere of Crown. However, without the Kingdom sphere it could not exist or continue to exist. This is an important realization; an important paradox. As the Universe is important to us, we are important to the Universe. In truth, we are co-partners and each state has its own executive qualities to live. From the Crown state of consciousness is the executive position to provide Allness and from the Kingdom state of consciousness, the executive position is to manifest Allness into the realm of matter. Therefore, it is the responsibility of each soul and each individual to manifest what Source provides.

The virtues that we use in this Sphere are Diagnosis and Discrimination. They help bring each person into the action of the executive position to manifest. To Diagnose, we are able to investigate and analyze the cause or nature of a situation or problem. This allows the ability to review our lives and decide what is growth-producing and what is not. It provides the ability to discern what needs to change in order to move to new levels. What changes assist in relieving pain or disharmony? Diagnosis helps identify any experience in order to deal with it properly. For instance:

+ Diagnose an illness to find its cure

+ Diagnose an emotional discord to find its balance

+ Diagnose a thought in order to comprehend its meaning

+ Diagnose "this and that" in order to configure a plan for manifesting

The virtue of Discrimination is activated after diagnosis is used. Right discrimination provides positive assessment and the ability to set issues apart from outer referencing and enter the realm of inner referencing. It is from this process that transformation of any situation can occur. Most particularly, right discrimination is the ability to release whatever causes disharmony in one's life and creates nonproductive activity. It provides the ability to set everything into a higher order above and beyond the limited view of 3rd Dimensional reality (blame, shame, negative judgment, lower ego, abandonment, betrayal and other illusions of being entrapped by the essence of others or the Collective Conscious). The ability to use diagnosis and discrimination is essential for achieving compassionate detachment and allowing self and others to find their way through the maze of life experiences without interference.

The Vices of the Kingdom Sphere are Inertia and Avarice. Inertia is the state of a body remaining inactive unless acted upon by some external force. Inertia causes a lack of motivation needed to take advantage of opportunities for growth.

It creates the repetition of the same or similar experiences circling in one's life without positive benefit. The swing of polarities occurs without achieving balance. Ups and downs, compulsions without direction and addictions occur as one attempts to find the center point of harmony. Being un-empowered and living in a path of darkness creates the reaction of inertia and the feeling or belief that the wishes and desires of your higher consciousness cannot be attained. These issues can be healed by living in the power of discernment and by testing your Path of Truth, Faith and Right Action. Using the power of understanding that comes through the grace of Diagnosis and Discrimination can most definitely help heal the experience of inertia.

The second vice of this Sphere, Avarice or Greed, is the excessive or insatiable desire for wealth or gain. Of course, this reveals the belief in lack rather than the knowing of affluence. Though there is more than enough abundance and prosperity to experience in life, excessive desire is the opposite of the Grace of Abundance, which is always provided by Source Consciousness. It is neediness and belief that you cannot have wealth that turns personal consciousness to the state of Avarice. The vice is certainly not Faith, which is the knowing that you are abundant. Avarice is the opposite of Faith with greedy attitudes explored at all levels of human consciousness (emotional, mental and physical). However, the power of Faith, which is encoded in each soul, can assist personal states of consciousness to overcome the fears associated with needy, greedy emotions.

When we are lost in the lower realm of separation, Lack, Avarice and Inertia, there is a Divine Plan at work to help bring the independent nature of the soul into awareness of its wholeness. The Divine provides states of consciousness of angelic qualities to be called to the forefront. Each soul is given a Holy Guardian Angel to help reveal the truth that Humans are interdependent with higher realms of existence. Angelic guidance assists us in "remembering" our Divine Self. These overseers hold the matrix of intelligence and full potential intact until each person can take charge (dominion) in their own right.

Angels are messengers and Light Beings (Illuminated Consciousness). As we achieve dominion, we become Illuminated Consciousness and recognize our own Angelic substance. Then, we become messengers of the Most Holy and assist in maintaining the Matrix of Divine Plans manifested.

The ultimate guardian angel of Earth is Sandalphon, Overseer of the Consciousness defined in the Sphere of Kingdom. Archangel Sandalphon is considered the Angel of the Messiahs (the inheritors of the Kingdom of Source). "Messiah" is a Hebrew word that means "anointed." To anoint is to consecrate and make holy or declare sacred. Sandalphon anoints each person and declares each sacred. This act of anointing is the power that helps the individual remember who they truly are.

Sandalphon holds the archetypal pattern for Earth itself and is considered the "Holder" of the soul patterns of humanity. Another name given to Sandalphon is "The Approacher" as she listens to our cries and through the agency of feeling, brings us silent hope and assurance. She is approachable by all souls and reminds us there is a "better day" if we will but seek it. She assists each individual to aspire and express the Higher Self.

Mankind's four basic natures are active in this final sphere of light on the Living Tree. Each provides a state of consciousness that represents the Divine in Matter:

- ✦ Sense – strength, patience, trustworthiness and compassion
- ✦ Logic – intelligence, originality, spontaneity and humanitarianism
- ✦ Response – courage, nobility, leadership, confidence
- ✦ Intuition – creativity, ambition, transformation and regeneration

As honor, balance and integration of these basic natures occurs, the individual becomes aware of his or her Divine Self. The Living Tree of Life is clearly known and All that Is, is recognizable through the personal experiences of life.

A symbol of the Divine Human is called 'Adam Kadmon.' The Divine Human is derived from the Creative World where Divine Force is contained and patterns of perfect existence are known. Adam Kadmon represents Divinity contained in a vehicle similar to mankind. The Divine Human represents the Creator's pure pattern of the vehicle which is evolving to awareness of being.

In Illustration 11, the Divine Human is shown facing the Living Tree. First, this indicates that physical sight cannot be used to see the Divine. Humanity must grow from within to see or know the Divine. To go within, one must face the Tree and recognize their existence as the Tree.

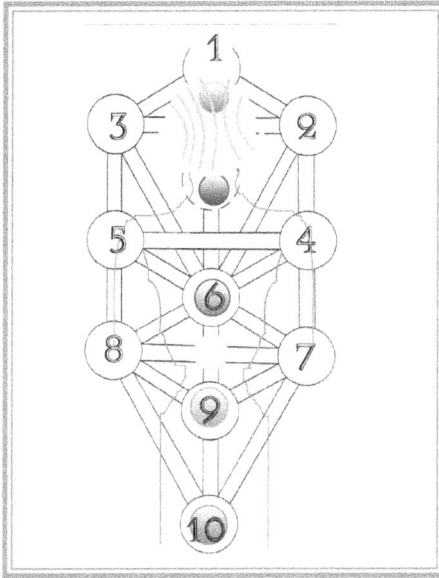

ILLUSTRATION 11: FACING THE INNER-MOST QUALITIES OF THE LIVING TREE

Facing the Tree, the left side (Receptive form) of the body receives the elements of the form of consciousness of the Tree of Life, while the right side (Active force) allows the expression of the Divine to be activated. This activation moves through the states of consciousness I have described as Worlds (Origination, Creation, Formulation and Manifestation) eventually formed 'Adam Protoplastes' or 'The First Human.' This is the first vehicle or body used as a human. As soon as this occurs, the journey of return was established.

The body-mind of the first human becomes refined by Individuation as his/her consciousness moves into higher levels of awareness (understanding the unknowable). Flexibility is required to evolve to higher consciousness. One must be willing to become more flexible and adaptable to his or her soul's pattern as consciousness nears the Light as the journey into the Evolution of Oneness occurs.

What is seen in the figure of Adam Kadmon is the essence of our ability to utilize the tools of the Spheres and Pathways of consciousness to assist in Soul Evolution. Through the Spheres of Light, we can see how consciousness develops through the interactive body-mind of a Human Being. The top of the head is just below the Sphere, Crown. This Sphere pours forth perfection – the breath of life and stimulates the pineal gland and pituitary glands. The head itself is between Wisdom and Understanding, as well as the path of Imagination. This path represents a door for universal and personal creation to emerge from thoughts within our head. Wisdom is the right hemisphere and Understanding is the left hemisphere. The throat of the Divine Human is the Abyss (void that is filled by the words of knowledge bringing creation into existence as it passes through the door of creative imagination). Thoughts contained within words form vibrations. The vibrations of the words are the builders of existence or the void of existence.

The shoulders connect to the Spheres of Mercy and Severity. Shoulders and arms represent man's spiritual and creative levels upon which creation is based. Arms and hands are the active, creative members of the abstract and concrete mental planes that shape and form manifestation.

The heart of the Divine Human is centered in the Sphere of Beauty. This is the control center. Beauty and Harmony centralize life. This is the hub of the spiritual being – the spiritual center. Integration with the spiritual center allows everyone to live in harmony, peace and understanding.

The hips and legs connect to Victory and Splendor. The mental, emotional and physical levels of humanity support human existence and are the foundation of human existence. A human learns to walk upright using clear intellect, balanced emotions and physical strength. Fears and insecurity create a state of crawling on the Earth in an animalistic expression of survival. Each human must not wallow in the lower frequencies, but must stand upright, aware of their own power. Each individual must strengthen emotional, mental and physical qualities in order to stand erect in higher realms.

The generative system of the Divine Human is in the Sphere of Foundation. This is the power responsible for the continuity of life in any manifested world. It is the instinctive power to reproduce human form, creative continuity, commercial productivity, and so forth. Upon the Foundation is built the residence for the experiences of each lifetime. The Foundation carries the responsibility for continuity of life in any world. Continuity of life experiences change as mass consciousness changes and connects to its Higher Planes of Awareness.

The Sphere of Kingdom is seen to encompass the thighs and knees of the Divine Human with the feet planted in Earth – the final place of desires being manifested. The Kingdom sphere is represented at the thighs where stability and structure holds the world firmly in place through the Agency of Spirit. And finally, in this Sphere is the containment of mind and soul, active and ready to manifest the ideals of Source.

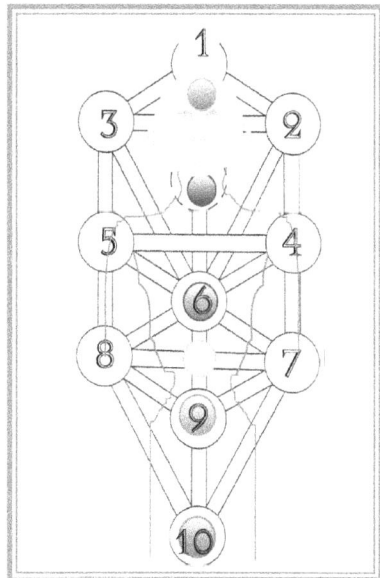

ILLUSTRATION 12:
FACING THE OUTER QUALITIES
OF THE LIVING TREE

Illustration 12 reveals the Divine Human facing outward, symbolizing the self-actualized human. The Human Being has taken the spiritual quest to journey within, has internalized, and utilizes the inner mysteries of Source. Universal wisdom and understanding is expressed through all living qualities of the individual. Oneness is understood, universal love is expressed. Life continues in the ebb and flow of higher awareness and the un-numbered and dotted sphere of Knowledge can be filled in.

How Sacred the Earth is, and its inhabitants.
It is the total reflection, expression and being of the Divine.
The Heart of the Divine beats within it.
The Heart of every soul beats within it.
We must learn that the Love of Living on the Earth is our
Ultimate Goal along with the Honor to Source:
God/Goddess – Our Self. All is One.

Part V

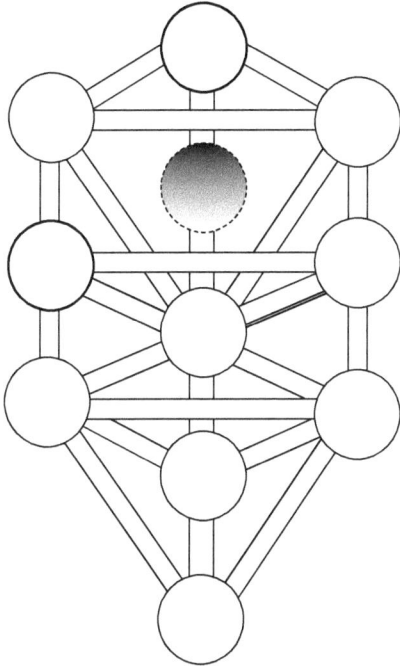

The Final Sphere: Abyss

The Power of the Sphere of Knowledge –
The Abyss

Though this Sphere is near the top of the Tree and not truly connected to a Triad, it is the last sphere to understand. It is the footstool of the Throne of Source and holds the foundation of all existence.

The Sphere of Knowledge is steeped in mystery. It is also called "The Abyss." It is depicted as a dotted line from the philosophy that we have not filled it with our intent to remain in states of Spiritual Integrity that are necessary to hold the purpose of its highest level. Yet I believe that in our Evolution of Union, we have been forming the right use of this sphere of consciousness. We have moved beyond the closed doors of secret mystery schools and opened to the wisdom of the Divine that is always available. We are maturing in our consciousness and becoming the Source that we already are; and completing the circle and becoming more aware of what this Sphere has to offer.

Known as "The Abyss," this Sphere was considered the great void and a fearful place for the novice to connect with or meditate on. In truth, we can only advance according to what we do know. We do not have the ability to examine or research that which we are unable to realize. Thus, The Abyss is not available to the individual who is not ready to comprehend the Great Knowledge that this Sphere has to offer.

To reach the Sphere of Knowledge, we must respond to the still small voice of our Soul and realize it is the goal of the Soul to be in perfect harmony with all knowledge. It is the intent of our Soul to maintain a Higher-Self Awareness and Actualize our Source Self through our Personality. As we grow into this awareness, we comprehend the greater wisdom of the Universe and rightly use it through our personal, creative processes. We integrate the Truth of Source with our personal truth in the Sphere of Knowledge. As we journey through levels of awareness and surrender to the higher states of conscious living, we transform many levels of our being and utilize the framework of wisdom to gain even greater knowledge.

We begin this journey of transformation by questioning what the knowledge of Source is. After receiving insight, we ponder the wisdom and set it in place in our automatic consciousness. We render it evident through the power of inner knowing. Then, we become enlightened and aware of the Creative Force behind all life. We comprehend this Creative Force and realize we are one with it and able to use it at all times. We become one with the Source that we have believed was a separate entity in the heavens somewhere far away from us. We discover it in us.

Knowledge offers the power to unfold within ourselves that which was spoken by Avatars (A divine being in earthly form, i.e., Buddha, Krishna, Christ, Enoch, St. Germaine). "The works that I do shall you do; and *greater works* than these shall you do." Why is this spoken? Because every soul that evolves to their higher self has a greater energy of conscious awareness available to them. Thus, wisdom is released and knowledge is fulfilled. Each time one individual reaches such a state, the wisdom infiltrates the collective conscious of all souls. Thus, this knowledge becomes easier for each person to access because of those who have journeyed the path before them. Those who journey on this wisdom path open the doorway of the great mysteries and allow more conscious awareness to evolve for all. Thus, the capacity for the human mind to comprehend the mysteries has become more advanced. This decreases the need for superstition (no more throwing spilled salt over the left shoulder or fearing seven years of bad luck when a mirror breaks). The capacity to comprehend the greater mysteries opens personal experiences to the understanding of the greater truth.

It is easy to observe that the growth of humanity has occurred with the greater state of personal and spiritual awareness as we comprehend our mental, emotional, physical and ego-states. We use more personal strength and intent to expand than we ever have before, at least in the last five thousand years. We expand our minds through many educational modalities, including the Internet, a relatively young modality (only brought into public use in the 1980s).

The Sphere of Knowledge is an internet. It is the matrix of all wisdom and is explored by spiritual desires to know more about the Creator. It represents the development of our higher consciousness as we display our ability to connect and live constantly from our Source Self. As we live in harmony and balance, greater realizations and awareness of our Source Self occurs and allows the next stage of our ascension to be recognized. We reveal, through human form, the Light of Source. In this state we know and are:

+ Genuine (truly what is said or done is authentic, sincere and honest)

+ Essential (recognize we are absolutely necessary)

+ Pure (a complete, unadulterated, paradigm of Wholeness)

+ Expressing the perfect pattern of Creation

Knowledge is awareness. Awareness is the ability to show knowledge with direct and intuitive cognition and synthesization of Soul intention. We render evident the Creator within. When we are in this state, mysteries are revealed, balance occurs, intelligence expands and the holy grail is discovered (soul container) revealing our purpose. The virtue of Spiritual awareness is vitalized. Doubt and corruption end. Compassionate detachment reigns as individuals comprehend that every other being is on their own path discovering Source. No matter what the path looks like, it is perfect. The Rainbow Bridge is recognizable. All people, circumstances and events are of the One Great Light reflecting through the prism of multitudinous expressions. Every act of living is the Covenant, the great agreement between the highest state of consciousness and the most dense state of consciousness (Source and Soul).

This sphere reveals the Will of the Indivisible Force of Higher Mind, the Essence of Source. It is the permanent archetype of Wholeness. It is the duality of the positive and negative forces synthesized. Living within this realm of consciousness, we activate a Higher Power and move into states of 'clairgnosis' (knowing) and graduate to more succinct spiritual awareness. After graduating through our awareness of external manifesting and strong sensate abilities, we are ready to enter the realm of Spirit and know our purity. To know a new level, we must graduate from the old level, detach from it (while retaining the awareness and understanding achieved) and fully involve ourselves in a new arena of education. Where are we now?

One of the means of telling where we are is to look at mainstream events. Check out our advertisements, television programs, most popular books (particularly self-awareness books) and even the changes in religious dogma. Our advertisements and television programs are more open than ever before. Our most popular books for self-awareness bring

everyone into a language of oneness. Science and spirituality are merging with the gifts of wisdom shared by quantum
theorists, archeologists and philosophers. The studies of the
Tree of Life are becoming predominant.

In the 1980s, it was difficult to find a teacher who would
speak of 'Qabalah' or 'The Tree of Life.' One only entered
the study in mystical schools. In 2000, it was on the lips of
everyone, even if it was part of a judgment against a singer
or movie star who had joined the ranks of its philosophy.
Today it is easy to access, and if dedication is used to uncover
the mysteries of the Living Tree, then the wisdom released is
life-changing. Yes, the Sphere of Knowledge is spilling out
its wisdom for all to glean. Why? Perhaps, it is because the
masters of the path have paved the way for others to enter
into this knowledge-based state of consciousness.

As with all other spheres of consciousness, an Archangel
is given charge to watch over the matrix and release the wisdom. In this Sphere, Archangel Tophiel is the active guardian. He is the teacher of mysteries. He reveals the truth that
we can know higher states of consciousness and the mysteries by the disclosure of knowledge through Divine means –
Union with Source Consciousness. Tophiel lets it be known
that truth must come from within and cannot be gained by
external realities. He reveals that intuitive capabilities are
the natural flow of wisdom. Contained within wisdom is
the truth that provides the empowerment of developing our
full potential. Archangel Tophiel reveals that Will or Intent
enables us to use information of the greater knowledge of
our full potential and materialize it in our daily existence on
Earth.

From the connection of personal consciousness to this
sphere of consciousness, Universal wisdom and understand-

ing is expressed through human realities. It is internalized in every cell of our body. We uncover it through Right Intelligence discovered through the expansion of the mind and opening of the heart. This heart-mind intelligence is accessed when we get beyond our personal awareness and marry our personal mind with the Divine Mind.

To enter the higher awareness and live through Divine Mind, we must sacrifice the old patterns through personal assessment, understanding and wisdom and allow true knowledge to emerge. We simply must use the innocent mind of curiosity and be willing to "not know" anything in order to know everything. Our deepest and most sacred state of conscious, Spiritual and Mystical consciousness opens. The rhythm and power of total wisdom is released. We know the Formless Form and the Sacred Heart. We become One and our awareness expands to the reality that We Are the Living Tree. The Life Force coursing through us is the vibrant capability to know, live, change, manifest, let go and begin again. No judgment, no fear, just the living power of evolution through the multitude of experiences.

Part VI

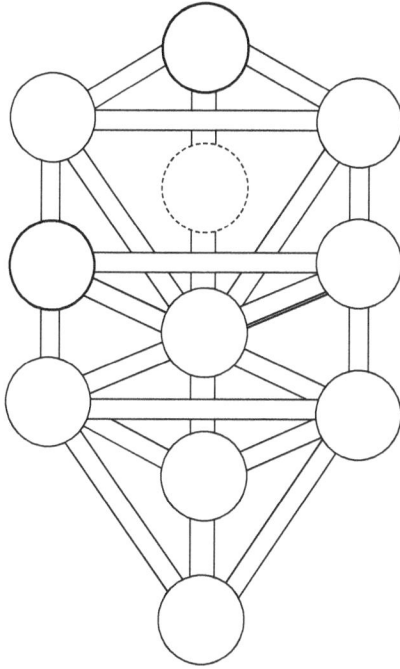

You Are the Living Tree

If you have followed the Spheres of Universal Wisdom and recognize the pathways you are blazing, perhaps this has been a journey of a lifetime for you. If you stayed on your pathway with the intention of truly knowing yourself, the universe and your ability to create what you really want in all areas of life, then this journey has been a fulfilling one for you.

I hope the studies that you have undertaken have provided you another level of comprehension of spiritual awareness. Perhaps it has opened the doorway to a deeper understanding of what you thought you knew. Hopefully, the wisdom you have gathered will be enhanced as you further your states of empowerment; simply because the Tree of Life has helped you open doorways of thought to higher realities, confirmation of your inner knowing, and the authentication of courage that allows you to seek, question and find the answers to complex concepts of Source.

Thank you for allowing me to be a Light Bearer on your Path of study through the Tree of Life. I am honored by your dedication and heart-expanded attitudes that have allowed you to uncover a wisdom that I find profound in bringing spiritual teachings under one "branch" of comprehension.

I pray you have found a new way to understand how all things are manifest. Of course, I pray that you have a new realization of the pairing of Source Consciousness with your individual consciousness and recognize that it is One Consciousness creating many experiences.

From the Crown to the Manifest world, I hope you are feeling the course of life continuing its ever-changing, always manifesting realities. You are in the stream of this energy of Creator Consciousness and you are an instigator of its flow. Your thoughts, emotions and actions direct the course of life.

Your ability to be clearly aware of what you are doing with your T.E.A. allows you to form the empowered state of the T.E.A.M. and your manifestations truly reveal what you desire and what Source desires.

May every branch, fruit and flower be lit on your Tree. May each light continue to guide you through deeper and greater wisdom.

Bibliography

Bletzer, Ph.D,, June G. (1987), T*he Donning International Ency-clopedia Psychic Dictionary,* Norfolk, VA. The Donning Company, Publishers.

Builders of the Adytum Mystery School, Independent studies, Los Angeles, CA.

Davidson, Gustav (1971), *A Dictionary of Angels, Including the Fallen Angels,* New York, NY: Free Press.

Fortune, Dion (1989), *The Mystical Qabalah,* York Beach, ME: Samuel Weiser, Inc.

Goodwin, Malcolm (1990), *Angels, An Endangered Species,* New York, NY: Simon and Schuster.

Gonzales-Wippler, Migene (1987), *A Kabbalah for the Modern World,* St Paul, MN: Llewellyn Publishers.

Gray, William G. (1987), *The Ladder of Lights,* York Beach, ME: Samuel Weiser, Inc.

Lamsa, George M. (1968), *HOLY BIBLE, From the Ancient Eastern Text,* New York, NY: Harper & Row, Publishers.

About the Author

REV. KATHERINE TORRES, PH.D., D.D.

From early childhood, Katherine has been a Seeker of wisdom of the Creator. Interaction with a world beyond the Earth was common for her and she only learned later in life that it was not common for all people. This encouraged an even deeper search to know and understand why.

Always seeking to be One with God, a mission in Katherine's heart was born. Education turned to the study of psychology and metaphysics. Eventually, the two merged and spiritual psychology became her pursuit. Holding a doctorate in Transpersonal Psychology, a doctorate in Holistic Astrology and many other certifications, Katherine Torres reaches out with her inner gifts and life education to help others.

Many years of spiritual and arcane studies and experiences led her to the study of Qabalah through the mystical school called 'The Builders of the Adytum.' Further studies ensued through a few teachers and many books. The gift of awareness of the Tree of Life mysteries was transforming. In fact, Katherine found an answer for healing problems of mind, body and soul in her own life. Excited about the wisdom and how it can help an individual pursue and manifest their desires through the awareness of their Source-Center, Katherine began teaching others how to use the wisdom of

The Tree of Life.

Over 46 years ago, a mystical experience created the pursuit of sacred wisdom that has compelled her to follow the mission of helping others help themselves. Her business, Transpersonal Development, was established as her ministerial status was confirmed in 1986. Since then, she has provided counseling, coaching, teaching, lecturing and writing as a means to inspire.

Visit her websites for further information: www.facesofwomanspirit.com, for classes, workshops and monthly insights; www.ignitethelight.net for Life Coaching inspiration; and www.spicawayoflight.com to discover a higher educational University of Divinity.

www.ingramcontent.com/pod-product-compliance
Lightning Source LLC
Chambersburg PA
CBHW051957090426

42741CB00008B/1427